THE YELLOW FOOTPRINTS TO HELL AND BACK

THE YELLOW FOOTPRINTS TO HELL AND BACK

The starting point for every Marine: a drill instructors' story of life in Marine Corps boot camp during the Vietnam War.

Gregg Stoner

iUniverse, Inc.
New York Bloomington Shanghai

THE YELLOW FOOTPRINTS TO HELL AND BACK
The starting point for every Marine: a drill instructors' story of life in Marine Corps boot camp during the Vietnam War.

iUniverse books may be ordered through booksellers or by contacting:

iUniverse
1663 Liberty Drive
Bloomington, IN 47403
www.iuniverse.com
1-800-Authors (1-800-288-4677)

Because of the dynamic nature of the Internet, any Web addresses or links contained in this book may have changed since publication and may no longer be valid.

The views expressed in this work are solely those of the author and do not necessarily reflect the views of the publisher, and the publisher hereby disclaims any responsibility for them.

ISBN: 978-0-595-48422-5 (pbk)
ISBN: 978-0-595-50120-5 (cloth)
ISBN: 978-0-595-60513-2 (ebk)

Printed in the United States of America

I dedicate this book to my beautiful wife Melody who was with me from the very beginning and supported me in every way possible; and my lovely daughter Erika who had to listen to my endless stories about "back when …" Without them this story would not have come about.

CONTENTS

INTRODUCTION

This book was written to tell a story about my unique experience while I was in the Marine Corps. The entire duration of my two enlistments, totaling five years, took place in a boot camp environment. I went from being a private in boot camp, to being a sergeant drill instructor in only nineteen months.

The period of time my story took place was during the Vietnam War, right after the largest invasion of South Vietnam, the Tet Offensive, had occurred. The American public was totally against the Vietnam War, and the young men that joined the Marines with me, all felt the same: we did not want to be involved with that war, but we had no choice. Most of us were going to be drafted by the Selective Service anyway. Unless we declared ourselves "conscientious objectors", and had the ability to prove it, we were all destined to go into combat. After all, the Marines exist to fight wars.

Instead of being sent to Vietnam, like all those I went through basic training with, I ended up being sent back to Marine Corps Recruit Depot, Parris Island, South Carolina. I did not get assigned a simple desk job that most clerk typists got, but rather, was assigned to a position at the Drill Instructor School as the chief clerk of the school. It was there that I obtained an education about the Marine Corps that many Marines don't get during a career in the Corps. I was surrounded by the top drill instructors, and leaders, that the Marine Corps had to offer. I was witnessing first-hand how drill instructors were trained, and what leadership skills were required for that role. It did not take school staff long to mold me into a different mind-set than when I first joined: my original goal was to go into administration, and not go to Vietnam. They lit a fire in me to experience the leadership of being a drill instructor.

I rolled the dice and took a significant chance by re-enlisting for three more years, with the privilege of attending the Drill Instructor School at Marine Corps Recruit Depot, San Diego. Had I failed the training, I would have certainly been sent to Vietnam, which was totally against my goals about that war. My wife and I relocated back to San Diego, and I went through the school. I was competing with career Marines that were all combat veterans; most had lots of decorations and medals for various acts of bravery. I was still feeling the pangs from boot camp, and yet, there I was being trained to be a drill instructor.

Upon successful graduation from the Drill Instructor school, I was given the unbelievable task of replacing my own drill instructor in the same company and platoon series I had graduated from only 19 months earlier. While there have been some prior cases of Marines being given the assignments of drill instructor duty shortly after they graduated from boot camp, my short time from boot camp to being a drill instructor was a modern day record during that time.

The Vietnam era was a unique era in Marine Corps and American history. It was the most unpopular war ever, and the American public, youth in particular, were vehemently opposed to it. The recruits that came in during that time were all from the baby boomer generation. They were spoiled, overly protected young men, many of whom had participated openly in protests of the war movement. They were often high from drugs upon their arrival, and most had heavily participated in the drug culture of those times. They presented a challenge to train. The war effort created a shortened training schedule, and that prompted many harsh techniques to break down the recruits, and remold them into United States Marines. This book describes the attitudes of the Baby Boomers, how those attitudes were molded, and the impact on training recruits.

During my time on the drill field I had many odd and interesting things happen. Some of those stories are truly hard to believe, but they happened exactly as I have written them. I wanted to give perspective on boot camp, as well as being a drill instructor, and my experiences qualify for that perspective.

Having fulfilled my second enlistment obligation, I left the Marines in pursuit of riches in the private sector. The money was certainly better, and there was not much chance of coming home in a body-bag, but civilian life was nowhere near as fulfilling as my special Marine Corps job. I had to make a major adjustment to civilian life and its general lack of discipline I was accustomed to in the Marines.

More than twenty years after I left the Corps I became associated with the Marines again by becoming a member in the United States Drill Instructor Association. After a few years of attending events and the annual reunions, I became the Secretary on the Board of the Crow Crawford chapter of the Marine Corps Drill Instructor Association. I now have the experiences of dealing with top-level Marine leaders, retired and active, who have all spent similar times as I being a drill instructor.

This book was written to tell my unique story, and to convey the feelings, and attitudes that dominated that special time in America, and how they affected recruit training. Anyone that was in the Marine Corps, past or present, will identify with the stories. Those that have not had the privilege of being a Marine will be amazed by some of the experiences told about in the book.

Semper Fi.

PART ONE:

BOOT CAMP

THE VIETNAM ERA AND
THE BABY BOOMERS

The Baby Boomer generation started in 1946 following the end of World War II. It began the largest bulge in population this country, and the world, had ever seen. "Boomers" were destined by their mass to change the way the world operated.

Through the 1950's life was pretty blissful for the Boomers. Moms usually were stay-at-home moms, and dads worked all day. Single parents were not as common as today. Things began to change in the 1950's: music was one primary area of change, with Rock and Roll becoming a major force by the end of the 1950's, and due to the size of the Boomers' mass, was destined to play a role in the following decades' changes.

The Cold War instilled a chilling reality to young Boomers. Schools practiced atomic bomb drills—diving under the desks to protect against the atomic bomb blasts that were anticipated as a possibility at any time. Air-raid sirens were tested at 12:00 PM every Monday: an eerie sound that filled the still air. Constant fear of the communist threat was part of our daily life. Boomers were raised under a constant cloud of fear that belied the bliss around them.

The 1960's roared into Boomers' lives, and by that time, they were becoming a teenaged mass. Anyone who has been around teens for any length of time, during any era, knows full well that a teenager is going through major changes in their bodies. Hormones flowed creating raging and abrupt patterns of behavior. Teens want to be independent, and break away from their parents' hold on them. But things were more different than at any time in the past. The massive size of the Boomers' movement was something that was destined to make change in America.

The Cuban missile crisis in the early 1960's put an additional chill into the world. Boomers were realizing that the atomic bomb drills that were common in the 1950 classrooms were becoming a reality they might have to deal with. The fact that the world came within a blink-of-an-eye of going into World War III with an atomic war became a stark reality. Boomers were taking note—that was not the way things should be.

President Kennedy was assassinated on November 22, 1963. That moment remains etched in the minds of every Boomer in America. Never in our lifetime had we had such a shocking event occurred. But, more than the shock of the assassination itself, was the shock of the apparent cover-up of the events, and the total mishandling of the evidence and witnesses. Big government was beginning to look very untrustworthy to youth. Questions of a possible conspiracy arose, compounding the mistrust. At a time when youth begins to question authority, the government was giving them a full platter of trust issues to deal with. Boomers were not happy with that at all.

The Beatles came upon the scene, and music was forever changed. Music became an area of solidarity for Boomers, and that music began to create a culture identity for them. "Independence" was their cry, and clothing reflected that independence with some outrageous styling, all prompted by their music idols. Long hair had become a means of showing contempt for the staid lifestyles of their adult counterparts. The drug culture was also taking shape, and youth was taking on a different avenue for recreational drugs than the alcohol their parents and elders had always used. The drug culture would make an enormous impact on the Boomers. The Hippy scene was in full swing as an anti-establishment movement.

Meanwhile, the U.S. government was taking a very active role in defending a small country in Southeast Asia called Vietnam. Most Americans had never heard of that country. America began to send advisory troops there to assist South Vietnam from the communist forces that were threatening them from North Vietnam. The number of troops sent there were small at first, but quickly catapulted to huge proportions as the 1960's raced on. Many people believed that the military-industrial complex was the root of the problem—war was big business, and if they could get a war going, then lots of goods and products would be purchased by the government, and big business would get richer. To justify their war, we were told of the dangers of communist growth, and of the need to stop that growth before it reached us. Somehow it did not seem right that a small nation on the other side of the planet could have any direct affect on us here in America: at least to the Boomers, that did not make sense.

During those times the military was not completely voluntary. They relied on the Selective Service drafting the personnel to make up their needs. That necessitated all young men, at the age of 17 years of age, to register with the Selective Service. Failure to do so was a crime that could result in imprisonment. More and more

Boomers were being drafted to fill the military's need. Deferments were possible for students in college, married men, and men with medical problems who were labeled as "4-F's". The rest were fair game. That was very chilling to most young men. The thought of being up-rooted from their lives to be sent to such a war somehow seemed untenable.

Just past the mid-point of the 1960's, President Lyndon Johnson escalated the war effort, and committed many thousands of U.S. troops to Vietnam. Although the war was not a declared war, we were in a full-fledged war none-the-less. Deferments for the Selective Service were curtailed, and they started taking married men, students with marginal grades, and other young men that previously were not allowed in the services. More than just an issue of being drafted became the issue that men were losing their lives in a war that they did not believe in. The public was never sold on that war in a way that previous wars had been accepted. That was exacerbated by the public also being given nightly news pictures of the graphic and horrific results of the war on prime-time TV. Never before in our history had a war been displayed to the public in such a manner. The viewers were horrified by what they were seeing.

The Vietnam was a jungle war. We were engaged with an enemy that did not play the war games the same way we were used to. Vietnam was hot and muggy, and the enemy often could not be discerned from the populace. The enemy could be *anybody*. It was not going to be a popular war for sure.

America was also engaged in problems on the home front. Civil rights were a major issue: protests were taking place across the nation to call out the inequities of the races. America was turning into a volatile arena for change. Laws were being enacted to give civil equalities to all people. But, it did not come without a price. During these times one of the principle leaders of the civil rights movement, Dr. Martin Luther King, was assassinated. Shortly afterwards, Senator Robert Kennedy was assassinated just after he had won the California Primary Election for the upcoming presidential election. America was in turmoil, and the war was a focusing point for most.

Music took on a new element of protest. Young people were buying into the protest movement in a major way. Students at colleges and universities were staging protests of the war, and violence was common. Men were dying in the battlefields for no viable reason as far as Americans, and Boomers, were concerned. The war was a travesty, and Boomers were the biggest losers of the war because it was they that were paying the ultimate price—dying for an unwarranted and losing cause.

As America got deeper in the Vietnam War effort the cost of American lives continued to rise dramatically. The death count was a daily news item during the prime-time telecasts. American people wanted out of that conflict, but it continued to go on. It was a never ending cycle: more troops sent to replace those lost in action. It seemed like every person in the country knew of at least one person or more that had either died in action, or was wounded, or maimed. The Vietnam War was getting very ugly.

In the beginning of 1968, the North Vietnamese struck a major blow to our presence there with the "Tet Offensive": an invasion of South Vietnam that caught us totally off guard. That was the turning point of major escalation of the war, and one of the darkest periods of American involvement in Vietnam.

President Nixon won the election in 1968 on a campaign aimed at getting the US out of the Vietnam War. But election promises were one thing, and ending the war was another. The war raged on. Boomers continued to die.

I was one of the baby boomers. I was caught in the current, and like everyone else, I could not escape.

THE YELLOW FOOTPRINTS

During the Vietnam War there were two paths to getting into the Marine Corps: some men were drafted against their will; some chose to join.

The draft was an evil in the 1960's. Being drafted was considered the kiss of death. Most draftees went into the US Army, and were generally shipped off to Vietnam after boot camp. Some draftees went into the Marines, and were also sent to Vietnam. Most Boomers did not want to be drafted, and were so opposed to Vietnam that many were willing to leave the country for Canada to avoid being drafted. Since Canada did not have a draft, they would not extradite young men to the US for draft dodging. While draft dodging was illegal, and could result in imprisonment upon capture, it was fairly common. However, even during that conflicted war, the dodgers of the draft were still cowards in most people's eyes. Being drafted was also a sign of failure: the person drafted had not been crafty enough to find an out.

In my case, I was in conflict with the war. I did not agree with it, and wanted no part of it. However, I was also of the belief that one did what was required, and being a draft-dodger was *not* an option. I was struggling in school, and I was hopelessly in love with my high school sweetheart, Melody. I was also heavily involved in hot rod cars: all of which took me away from my studies enough for my grades to slip, resulting in losing my deferment. Life seemed to be closing in on me, so I married Melody, and upon return from our brief honeymoon, I found a notice in my mailbox to take a draft physical. That was a major blow, as it most certainly would result in my being drafted, and then having to live the nightmare every Boomer wanted to avoid—fighting a war I did not believe in.

After taking my pre-draft physical, it was obvious to me that there were no physical reasons for the Selective Service to not draft me. During that time-frame it was typical that about three weeks from taking the physical, a draft notice would be issued, and just like that, you were in the military. I was not going to take that lying down.

My new bride and I went to the local recruiting office in downtown San Diego. Initially my game-plan was simple: I wanted to join the Navy reserves. Since San Diego was a Navy town, I figured that by joining the Navy reserves I would not be sent directly to Vietnam, and into a conflict that I could not endorse. I also thought that after a two year reserve enlistment, I would be out and back into civilian life again, but I would still be in the reserves for another four years. It seemed simple to me anyway. So, when we got inside the recruiting office I initially walked up to a Navy Chief who was sitting behind his desk, talking on the phone. His feet were on his desk, and he was leaning back in his chair. He was engrossed in a conversation with someone, and he continued to just ignore me and my brides' presence. On and on he talked.

"Can I help you young man?" asked a voice behind me. I turned, and sitting tall and erect at his desk was a Marine Corps recruiter in his dress blue uniform. He was squared away, and had a certain look of authority lacking in the Navy recruiter across the room. We walked over to his desk, and I told him of my plan to avoid being drafted, and that I wanted to enlist into the reserves to minimize my exposure. He told me that the Marines had no openings in the reserves, but had just come out with a new two-year enlistment plan that did not involve additional reserve time: it was the same as the draft. I told him that my desire was to be in some administrative capacity due to my having over two years of college, and that I definitely did not want to go to Vietnam. He laughed at my request and said "Son, this is the Marine Corps: what we do is fight wars, and *all* Marines go to Vietnam. Besides, with only a two-year enlistment I cannot guarantee you a specific billet. You would need to enlist for four years to get a guarantee." For some reason, and against all logic, joining the Marine Corps on a two-year enlistment made sense to me. Somehow I had a feeling that all would be well. So I signed up, on the spot, and elected for a two-month delayed entry. I would be following in my older brother Laurney, and my Cousin Harleys' footsteps in becoming a Marine. The two-month delay would give me time to make the adjustments I needed.

During the next two months I was given plenty of advice from friends, and family, on what, and what not to do at boot camp. "Don't let them learn your name." "Don't volunteer for anything." It went on and on. What I did get a lot was that Marine Corps boot camp was not going to be easy. Everything I heard magnified my fears of what to expect. Trepidation continued to grow by the day.

Finally, the day came to leave for the Marines. I had been given a Greyhound bus ticket to go from San Diego to the Los Angeles military processing center.

It was the same location where we had to take our draft physicals. The bus was to leave the depot at 4:30 AM sharp. The call to board the bus was given, and everyone began to board. I kissed my crying wife Melody goodbye, then boarded the bus. It was really hard to leave my bride of only three months, but that was the choice we had to make. The ride up was not eventful, but upon arrival to Los Angeles, the bus was stopped, and a military policeman came aboard the bus and said that there were protesters outside the facility, that they expected some trouble from them. We were taken to the rear entrance of the building.

The processing center was very dehumanizing. Another cursory physical took place requiring us to walk semi-nude around that huge building, following various colored lines on the floor. Each color went to a specific area. After that was over, and they hadn't found anything to disqualify us, we were put into a staging area to await the next step which was the oath. But, before they were ready to issue the oath, it was meal time, and everyone was given a chit to take to a nearby eatery called "Corky's". This place had to rate as one of the worst eating establishments in all of Los Angeles. It was a cafeteria that offered a variety of absolutely horrible food. The place was sleazy, the food looked bad, and the place smelled. It was so disgusting that one person in line simply threw his entire tray of food at a nearby wall, and declared that the process was totally inhumane. I suspect that he was a draftee, and was there against his will. I am also sure that the federal government must have had a big long-term contract with Corky's that allowed them to get away with that travesty of culinary dealings.

The oath was given by 2:00 PM, and we were quickly separated into our respective services. Army personnel went to one room, Air Force another, and so forth. All of the Marines were told, in our room, that we would shortly be getting on a bus to San Diego Marine Corps Recruit Depot, and the bus would be leaving soon. Another two hours later we were on board, and heading south toward San Diego. All those aboard faced the same fate for the next three months. I looked around to size up my peers: lots of young men with long hair, and all of them having the look in their eyes that was full of the unknown. Most talk was of the small-talk variety. Some were relaying their last minute advice from friends and relatives about what to expect. I don't think any of us really had a good idea. We only had vague ideas. The closer we got to San Diego, the quieter the group got.

Finally, the bus arrived at the main gate of Marine Corps Recruit Depot (MCRD). The sun was quickly going down. We all looked out our windows, and the reality was sinking in that we were now in the Marine Corps, and life was going to change. We were all a little awed by the sight of Marines standing in formations along our short bus route through the depot. The world seemed to change to a different color on that side of the gate. Our stomachs were getting tied in knots in anticipation of the unknown. The bus eased up outside a yellowish-colored building. Our hearts started to race.

From the yellow building walked a tall man in a dress blue uniform.—He looked really squared away, but more importantly, he looked *really serious*. On his way to the bus he passed four rows of yellow footprints, about 100 in total, in rows of 25 each. He entered the bus, and stood between the rows of seats, and said in a loud voice full of authority: "You are now in the Marine Corps, and will do everything you are told. You are to get off this bus as fast as you can, and run to one of the yellow footprints on the ground outside the bus. There you will stand with your hands at your sides and with your head and eyes straight to the front. You will say nothing until spoken to. I want to see nothing but assholes and elbows when you get off this bus. From now on, the first and last words out of your mouths will be 'sir'. Do you understand me?" "Sir, yes sir" we replied. "*Now get off the bus!*"

Whoosh. Nothing but assholes and elbows! It was hard to imagine a bus being emptied so quickly. We stood erect on the yellow footprints. All eyes straight ahead, hands at our sides. In front of us was a sign, high on a wall of the building, that gave the basics of the Uniform Code of Military Justice (UCMJ). These rules were quickly read to us. The most striking point was that we now did not have our civilian rights, and were subject to military justice.

Immediately after our indoctrination to Code of Military Justice, we were again informed that the first and last words out of our mouths were going to be "sir" from that point going forward. We were then ordered to run in columns up to the hatch (door) the Marine first came through. "Sir, yes sir!" we all bellowed, and then ran, in line, up to the hatch. Once there, we were ordered to file inside, and to jump into a barber chair. Our hair was shaved off in a matter of seconds. Once shaved, we were quickly routed to another room where we were told to take off all our clothes to get ready to take a shower.

Wow. We had been there less than 5 minutes, and already we had lost our most striking piece of identity: our hair. We then were standing naked next to strangers. Hearts raced. What was next? The Marine handlers were yelling and screaming at us to hurry up. That created chaos. We were told to get into a small room with about 40 other recruits, and take a shower. There were about 8 water spigots on the bulkheads (walls), and we all had to share a spigot. The whole time a Marine, who was standing in the doorway, was yelling for us to hurry up. As we left the room we were squirted with a de-lice spray, and then issued a towel to dry off. We had to run back to the cubicles where we had left our civvies. At that point we were herded through another area where we were issued our first clothing. We had to run past a Marine who quickly assessed our size, and threw a set of skivvies at us, as well as trousers, belt, yellow sweatshirt, a pair of sneakers, and socks. We rushed back to the cubicles to dress quickly. Everything seemed too big. Yelling was constant. The experience was turning into a nightmare.

Our next project was to make a box. When done, we were given a strict set of rules about what we could keep, and what was contraband. It seemed like almost everything was contraband. Everything we could not keep was to be put into the boxes. Then Marines came around and checked every single item we had kept out. More yelling ensued. Apparently some people did not understand the contraband part. Once the boxes were filled, we had to address the boxes to our homes, and then seal them up. That was the last remnants of our civilian lives we would be seeing for the next few months.

Once our boxes were sealed, they were stacked next to a wall. We were then herded out to another larger, open room, where we were told to sit on the floor, and await further word. We were not to say a word to anyone. The room was filled with silence except for the yelling and screaming taking place in other rooms nearby. We all wondered what was going on. We also began to wonder why we had ever placed ourselves in this situation. We waited and waited.

Most of us had not eaten much at Corky's, as the food was so bad. That meant that most of us had not eaten since very early that morning, if at all. It was getting to be very late at night, and we were all starving. Most of us also had not slept for 24 hours, or more. One does not get much sleep the night before going into the Marine Corps. So we all sat there, starving and fatigued beyond the experience levels we had encountered in our lives thus far. More and more recruits were ushered into the room we sat in, and we all continued to wait.

We were given a brief moment on occasion to use the heads (toilets). They meant a very *brief* moment, consisting of one minute, or less. During a visit to the head, I was surprised to see that the exposed plumbing was polished all the way up the bulkheads (walls). I could not help but think, that the Marine Corps was more anal about some things than I had envisioned. Everything was spic and span. *Everything!*

Soon the Receiving Barracks personnel were back in our room, hollering more orders to us. We were then ushered into another supply line where we were all issued what was known in the Marine Corps as the "Bucket Issue": a bucket, two sheets, a blanket, pillow, personal care items such as a shaving kit with toothpaste and toothbrush, scrub brush, laundry detergent, etc. We were given a heavy-duty deep bag made of nylon, with a strap to hang it over the shoulder, and were known as a "sea bag". The sea bag was to put the newly issued gear in. Once we were done cramming the gear in the sea bag, we were rushed back into the same room again, and ordered to sit on the floor. All that time the handlers were yelling, screaming, and making our lives instantly miserable. It was getting to be past midnight, and there was no end in sight. We were in total submission at that point.

Finally, after an eternity of waiting on numb rear ends, we were told to rise, and grab our sea bags. "Sir, yes sir" we answered in unison. Not good enough—"*I can't hear you!*" was the drill instructors reply. "*Sir, yes Sir*" we all screamed back again. We were told to run outside, and stand again on the same yellow footprints that we started off on. Again, one could see nothing but assholes, elbows, and a cloud of dust. Soon, about eighty-five to ninety recruits were standing on the footprints, hands at our sides, staring straight ahead. It was 0300 hours (3:00 AM). What was next we wondered? We would soon find out. These were the yellow footprints to hell and back.

A Marine wearing a Smokey-the-bear hat introduced himself as Staff Sergeant Hickman who told us he was going to be our Platoon Commander. He then introduced Staff Sergeant Troutman and Sergeant Christian who were the junior drill instructors. Then all hell broke loose, and they swarmed on us like stink on crap. Yelling and screaming. It was everywhere, and in stereo. "*Look straight ahead!*" "*Get your eyes off me boy!*" "*Stand straight with your hands at your side.*" Then the order: "Forward, march", and the platoon was off into the darkness. We went for what seemed like forever, meandering between buildings, across parking lots and parade decks. The whole time we were lugging those heavy sea bags loaded with all of our new possessions. The platoon pulled and pushed, and the drill instructors (DI's) were yelling every step of the way. We finally stopped outside of a row of metal buildings with domed roofs that curved all the way down their sides. The buildings were known as "Quonset huts", and they were to become our first housing while in the Marine Corps. Each of the four rows of recruits was known as a squad. The row I was in was the row on the right side, and it was the first row, so it was the "First Squad". Each squad was directed into a separate Quonset hut, and we were ordered to make up metal bunks known as "racks", with sheets, blankets etc. We were given two minutes to accomplish that task. Many of the young men appeared to have never made a bed up before in their lives, and that was a new deal for them. The drill instructors had no trouble finding those who were inept at the task, and getting right up into their faces with voices that were non-stop screaming. Once we had our racks made up, we were told to jump in them, and go to sleep. *Oh my God.* That couldn't be real. Everyone was shocked by the whole experience. Most of us were trying to figure out what could have possibly motivated us to put ourselves into that situation in the first place.

Everyone lay in their racks. The long march from the Receiving Barracks to our new Quonset huts, carrying our heavy issue of new gear, had taken the wind out of us. As tired as we all were, sleep did not seem to be possible for us. We just laid there. The feeling that we all had was that we just wanted to burst into tears. What on earth had we gotten into? We tossed and turned. An eternity seemed to go by, and then, out of total exhaustion, we fell asleep.

"Reveille! Reveille! Reveille! Get your asses out of those racks and get dressed!" the DI's yelled. They were pounding on the metal trash cans, and pulling recruits from their racks. What a shocking way to wake up. It was now 0430 (4:30 AM), and we were being woken after only a few minutes of sleep. It was time for a new day, and our first full day of Marine Corp fun.

SHOCK AND AWE:
WELCOME TO MCRD

When we first arrived at MCRD we brought with us all of the individuality we were raised with. We had become independent young men used to handling our own affairs our own way. It was important for the Marine Corps to break us of that individuality and start the process of getting us to think in terms of teamwork and being under a much disciplined order of doing things.

The hair cuts removed our individual image. Suddenly we looked like everyone else. When we put on our initial clothing issue we further looked like everyone else in our new platoons. We no longer possessed the look we came in with that bolstered our egos. Joe Willie Switchblade no longer looked his part—in fact, he looked gimpy. His clothes didn't fit, his shaved head was barren and suddenly he looked like a wimp. Nobody saw him as a tough guy anymore. In fact, nobody saw him at all.

By putting recruits into a mass shower we were introduced to communal living. Nobody had any secrets. We were completely stripped of any dignity we came in with and now were more open to a total restructuring. The whole ordeal at the receiving barracks was of a design to accomplish the tearing down of the egos.

The long walk to our new housing in the middle of the night was very disorienting. That disorientation put us more at the mercy of our drill instructors' orders. We were lost and needed a leader to pave the way. We were opening up more and more to this. Our lack of sleep to that point had exacerbated our fatigue and disorientation. Allowing us only an hour of sleep set a tone and began to show us that we would be going through a lot of changes going forward. Sleep was just one of them. Hunger would be another.

The introduction to the drill instructors was sort of the icing on the cake. Immediately we recruits realized that everything we had heard prior to coming to boot camp was *understated*. There were no words to describe this experience that a civilian who had not experienced this can really comprehend. These drill instructors were for real! The Marine DI was sharp as a tack. His trousers and shirt were creased with razor sharp edges. He was totally squared away with a high-and-tight haircut, chiseled look and a voice that boomed like nothing we had ever experienced. He stood in stark contrast to us recruits whose uniforms at that point was ill-fitted, unkempt, and overall, very frumpy looking. The DI was now king. There was no question about that. No question at all. At that point, the drill instructor could begin the slow process of evolution: from chaos to order. It would take many months to accomplish, but accomplish he would.

One of the first orders of things was for the DI's to set up the basic military protocols: how to speak, how to stand, to march, etc. These had to be accomplished before anything else. Every single facet of a our daily life was going to be re-taught from that point going forward.

In order to speak to a drill instructor it was first necessary for us to request permission to speak: "Sir, Private Stoner, Platoon 196, requests permission to speak to the drill instructor, sir!" Only after being given permission to speak could a recruit speak. In most cases the DI would reply: *"I can't hear you!"* necessitating that we had to start all over again, louder the next time. It was not uncommon for that process to take three or four attempts before the DI allowed us to speak.

The position of "attention" was the most basic position in the military. It required the feet to be positioned at a 45 degree angle with the heels together, the hands along the sides with the thumb parallel to the seams of the trousers and the head and eyes straight ahead. The body remained still. That was the very first position taught to recruits. As simple as it was it was often the most violated. It was not natural to keep our eyes straight ahead when the drill instructor was moving about and yelling—there was a tendency to want to follow the DI's movements. Establishing a discipline here was the first order for us to heed. The DI's were all over this lack of discipline. It would be an ongoing task to get that down correct.

Marching was another primary movement in the Marines. Marching was nothing short of organized walking, but done so in a very disciplined manner. Everyone was doing the exact same thing at the same time. Marching always started off with the left foot first. It began with the command: "Forward, March", and ended in the command "Platoon, Halt". Once these basic movements had been taught to us, we were marched off to the mess hall for our very first Marine Corps meal.

Before entering the mess hall for the first time the drill instructor told us how to proceed through the lines. We were told: "Take a tray, knife, fork, and spoon and proceed down the line. Put your tray out for any particular food items you want. Take all you want. Eat all you take. No exceptions. No talking in the lines or at the tables. Once done, take the tray to the drop area where it will be left for cleaning by the mess personnel. Get back outside and fall into formation and await the drill instructor."

Our first meal was breakfast. A typical Marine Corps breakfast consisted of a meat such as bacon, sausage or ham, scrambled eggs, toast or biscuits, cereal, various fruits and a specialty referred to as "SOS"—basically SOS was supposed to be a variation of chipped beef on toast, but had a sinister look to it and it was made with ground beef instead. For the inexperienced, this particular dish can look nauseating. It is not known as "SOS" (shit on shingles) for just any reason, after all. We were not allowed to have coffee—only milk or juice. Marine Corps chow was not exactly what someone would refer to as "home cooking", but it was filling and had the calories that would be needed for our daily training regimen.

During the first week we were at the depot we were going through the processing phase. This was for the purpose of getting our initial clothing issue, starting our inoculation process at the medical center, having vision tests, and going through intelligence testing. In addition, we are were issued our "782 gear" consisting of a rifle, cartridge belt, canteens, bayonet and other gear that would be needed to learn basics and get through boot camp training.

The DI's would virtually swarm on us recruits for every single little thing they found being done wrong—and there was never a shortage of things they could find being done wrong. As gangly recruits we were in total shock just about every minute of our first days in boot camp.

Processing week was one of the toughest for the us because we were deathly afraid of being singled out by the DI's for doing something wrong. Nothing was smooth for us yet. We were unsure about everything. My own experience was somewhat typical. My drill instructor, Staff Sergeant Troutman, was marching a small squad of recruits across the parade deck on the way to a vision exam. He stopped us on the parade deck for a moment to chew out a recruit for not being in step. His yelling and screaming were deafening and it invoked fear in all of us in the group. It was at this point that I realized that I had not brought my glasses with me, having left them in the footlocker at my Quonset hut. It would be necessary for me to let the DI know this so I could go back and get them for the eye exam. With all the courage I could muster I broke ranks and ran up to the drill instructor, stopping at the position of attention and then attempted to request permission to speak to the drill instructor as we had been informed to do. Instead of words coming out of my mouth, however, I found that I was so scared that my body froze, and my throat muscles would not respond. I was utterly incapable of making a sound! SSgt Troutman glared at me at first, and then began to scream at me which only made matters worse. I had an enormous muscle spasm in my throat—I can still recall that muscle tension to this day. After what seemed to be an eternity, all the while SSgt Troutman was hollering at me, I finally managed to squeak out "Sir, Private Stoner, Platoon 196, requests permission to speak to the drill instructor, Sir." With utter relief I was amazed that he simply said "Speak." I then made the fatal mistake of referring to myself in the first person which, in Marine Corps boot camp, was close to committing a criminal act: "Sir, I forgot my glasses in my footlocker, sir." At the top of his lungs his reply was *"I? Are you a private I? Who the hell is 'I'? Are you some sort of communist idiot that came here to screw around with me, Maggot Face?"* If feeling low can be described in honest terms, at that point I felt lower than dog poop on the pavement. I had to respond, but my throat was quickly cramming itself shut tighter than a drum. All I could respond with was "Sir, do you want me to go back and get them?" This was when I realized that I had just committed another very cardinal sin in Marine Corps boot camp—I referred to the DI as a "you". *"Do I look like a female sheep to you, Dipshit?"* the DI yelled. *"Do you want to make love to me, boy?"* he continued to scream. *"Sir, no, sir!"* I replied. I could see that this was going in the worst possible direction it could. Fortunately for me two more recruits stepped forward with the same problem. After a thorough chewing out, we were all sent back to the Quonset huts on the double to get our glasses. Already I wanted to just die on the spot, and we hadn't even begun the training phase yet. This was going to be a long saga for us. I decided that I was going to become as invisible as I could be for the remainder of boot camp to avoid direct confrontation with the drill instructors.

GET IN STEP

The Marine Corps takes pride in their presentation of close order drill. Drill was a means of instilling, and demonstrating, discipline. The title of "Drill Instructor" stems from the teaching of drill to recruits. Done properly drill can be like a ballet dance—smooth and artistic, like a well oiled machine. But, drill takes practice—lots and lots of practice to make it good. The process actually starts off very slowly.

Marching was the process used in the Marines to get a unit from one place to another. It starts with the command "Forward, march", and everyone steps off with their left foot first, and continue at a pace of 120 steps per minute. Each step being done simultaneously with everyone else. When the drill instructors first teach marching, they use a very slow cadence, so that everyone gets used to marching "in step" with everyone else. It seems easy to say. But in reality getting eighty-five to ninety recruits to be "in step" with each other was no easy task. Recruits were under a lot of stress when they first arrived at boot camp. The drill instructors were constantly yelling, screaming, and making sure that the recruits were off-balance all the time. Nobody wanted to mess up because they knew they would face the consequences of the drill instructor getting into their faces. Having a DI in your face was like having a Doberman pincher growling just inches from your nose. Your heart skips a beat, and your pulse nears the explosion level.

Recruits tried very hard to do what they were asked to do, but sometimes their efforts were in vain, as they were misreading a queue, and didn't know it. My own experience was a good example. About two or three days into the first week at boot camp, during processing week, my drill instructor Sergeant Christian, was marching our platoon across the parade deck. Our pace was slow—left, right, left, right. Sergeant Christian was calling out the cadence in a fairly loud, and clear manner. My brain was locked on the commands—left, right, left, right. The recruit in front of me was marching the opposite of me with his steps—I was immediately aware of the problem, and thought to myself "Oh my gosh, this guy's going to get killed in a minute." Sergeant Christian yelled out at the top of his lungs: "*Get in step maggot!*" The private ahead of me continued his pace opposite of mine. Again, I said to myself: "You're in for a bruising, private: you should get in step before he comes over here." Still the recruit was opposite steps with me, and suddenly, Sergeant Christian was walking our way, yelling louder, and cursing "*Get in step you little shit!*" Nothing changed. Intensity was growing. I could only imagine the outcome when this was over, and it was right in front of *me* no less. Finally Sergeant Christian gave the platoon the command to halt. He was getting closer to us, and was yelling "*I told you to get in step you little shitbird!!*" He then walked directly up to *me*, and punched me square in the chest, and said "*Next time I tell you to get in step, you get in step—do you understand Maggot-Breath?*"

I had been so confidant that I was in the right, and the recruit in front of me, as well as all the others, were out of step, that it never occurred to me that it was *me* that was out of step, not them. That lesson would stay with me for life: never be so bold as to not think that you might be the one that is out of step. Always be open to the fact that you *might be wrong*.

THE SMOKING LAMP IS
LIT FOR ONE CIGARETTE

I was a smoker when I enlisted in the Marines. I was used to smoking about a pack of cigarettes per day, and that was pretty normal smoking activity in those days for the average person. Cigarettes were pretty cheap back then—around 30 to 35 cents per pack in a store. Smoking was known to be bad for your health, but everyone pretty much ignored those warnings. It was cool to smoke. Looking back at any movie from those times you will see that all the stars in the film smoked. It was the thing to do, and a vast majority of Americans enjoyed the habit.

When we first arrived at MCRD we were deprived of all personal luxuries that we were used to having as civilians. We were going to go through an abrupt change in our daily lives that required us to not have any of the things that we had grown accustomed to having to ease our tensions. Smoking was one of those.

With all of the activity that we were forced to endure those first few days, we did not have too much time to fret over not having a smoke. But, for those of us who had smoked habitually, not having a cigarette was a very stressful draw on our body's desires. It was especially more difficult after eating a meal, as this was when a cigarette seemed to have its best taste and affect. However, with a mad-man drill instructor running around yelling at us, cursing at us, and keeping us moving all the time, we just kept moving on without them. But it was a thought that kept us going—when will we ever get a smoke?

Over a week went by without smoking a cigarette. I was beginning to conclude that it would be the perfect time to stop smoking. By that time my body had become more or less accustomed to not smoking, and I felt that it was the perfect opportunity to quit the ugly habit once and for all. The situation was perfect for that. I was becoming at ease with the thought of it.

One day in the middle of my second week at boot camp, shortly after the dinner meal was done, we were back in our area squaring it away, getting ready for the evening activities. We heard our drill instructor say something, and were we not sure what he meant: "The smoking lamp is lit for one cigarette." What does he mean by "the smoking lamp"? Someone jumped up, and said "Hey, that means we can smoke!" Everyone ran to their footlockers, pulled out a cigarette and a lighter, and ran outside to fall into the formation that was forming. Sergeant Christian was in front of the group. Again he said "The smoking lamp is lit for one cigarette. And I mean only *one cigarette!* Anybody that does not smoke is to return to your Quonset hut and continue what you were doing." We all reached for the cigarettes we held, and lit one as soon as we could. I could not believe how good it felt. I got a buzz from it almost immediately, and continued to feel light-headed while I puffed away. Life was taking on some meaning at last. All of my thoughts about quitting the habit went out the window in a flash. That was the first pleasure I had in over a week and a half. I could not help but wonder where the term "smoking lamp" came from—none of us dared ask.

While we smoked, Sergeant Christian explained to us that smoking was a privilege in the Marine Corps, and that the privilege was only allowed when they authorized it. In addition, he explained that once we were done with the cigarette, we had to "field dress it", which meant to extinguish it, and then remove the ash by rolling it in our fingers, and placing the butts in our pockets. He made it crystal clear that at no time would a butt on the grounds be acceptable. That was the way Marines took care of their areas, he explained. All one had to do was to look around the base, and it was obvious that it was spic and span in every location—unlike civilian areas that have trash flying, and cigarette butts on the ground.

It was not long before the recruits that did not smoke realized that smoking was the only privilege that recruits were going to get. I was somewhat amazed to see some non-smoking recruits suddenly take up the habit just so they could enjoy some type of privilege. It seemed very odd, but as long as the smoking lamp was there we had something to look forward to.

From that point on the smoking lamp was lit usually three times per day, most often after our meals were done. One thing we knew—if we screwed up it was not going to be offered. We had a carrot to chase.

There were some of the privates in my series that just felt they could get away with sneaking a smoke. For those people, controlling their desires was hard for them to do, even in a Marine boot camp environment. You would think that just the thought of the potential consequences of violating a basic order would be enough to stop anybody from doing so. But, there were those that violated these orders—it was the job of the drill instructors to catch them.

Catching recruits smoking was fairly easy—after all, the smoking lamp was only lit while they were in group formations, so smoke rising from an area that was not a formation was a quick tip off that somebody was smoking a cigarette. The most common place to sneak a smoke was in the heads late at night. After taps, things got quiet. Recruits, as well as drill instructors, were in bed. The only people moving about were the recruits standing guard duty, walking through the area. Occasionally the Officer-of-the-Day came through, but rarely in the middle of the night. Recruits also had free access to the heads one hour after taps, and that was often when recruits went there. They could have some degree of privacy since there was often nobody there at the time. They could relax, and spend a few moments on the commode. It didn't take too many nightly trips to the head around 2400 (midnight) to realize the lack of apparent scrutiny there. A light would go off in their heads: "Why not smoke a cigarette then? After all, who was here to catch me?"

The heads back then were wooden buildings that were about forty feet long by thirty feet wide, and were made sometime back before World War II. They had rows of about 12 commodes against each bulkhead (wall) on the exterior side bulkheads, and there was a six foot high bulkhead directly down the center of the building that had urinals on both sides of the bulkhead. A recruit could feel pretty safe sitting in the rear commode smoking a cigarette. But, they always forgot one little thing—drill instructors were very cunning, and had been there before! It was not uncommon for a DI to climb up to the rafters of the head, and wait for a victim to arrive. The recruits just never seemed to look up at the ceiling. Once the recruit lit up, the drill instructor would jump down, and from that point, the recruit was going to be toast.

"So you like to smoke do you, private?" the drill instructor would ask. "Sir, yes sir" was the standard reply. *"Good. Go get your smokes and your bucket and be back in 45 seconds flat!"* The recruit would run to his hut, and come back in seconds with his pack, a lighter, and his bucket as ordered. The DI would order: *"Now put seven cigarettes in your mouth, and light them."* Quickly, the recruit would stuff the seven cigarettes in his mouth, and light them all. *"Place the bucket over your head, and smoke those cigarettes down to the filters"* The drill instructor would command. It did not take long for the expected result to take place: with a heavy supply of smoke filling the bucket air space, and the seven cigarettes inserted between the lips, the recruit would very quickly become nauseated, and pretty overcome with the lack of clean air to breath. In many cases these were the last cigarettes a recruit

would ever smoke—they usually could not ever bear again to inhale another whiff of smoke.

Today the Marine Corps has changed the smoking policy to eliminate recruits from smoking altogether. They also do not allow those drill instructors who smoke, to smoke in front of the recruits. Having stopped smoking many years ago, I feel that this was absolutely the best course of action, for the health reasons alone. But I also cannot help but think back to joy of those days when the smoking lamp was lit for one cigarette

WHERE'S THE STICK?

One of the most basic items we dealt with was our footlocker. The footlocker was a wooden box that was roughly three feet wide, by two feet tall, and two feet front-to-back. It had a hasp on it, and it was to be locked at all times with a combination lock that was issued to the recruit at the receiving barracks. Each Quonset hut or barracks the recruit lived in at all of the facilities of recruit training had a footlocker under their racks.

All of our worldly possessions while in boot camp were kept in our footlocker. It was *our domain*. There was a prescribed order to the footlocker that we had to keep our clothing and personal items in. It was not just a dumping-off point to cram our stuff into. If we were lucky, our footlocker would have a tray that sat inside the top part of the locker, and we could keep our smaller personal items such as our tooth brush, soaps, and the like. If not, then we kept those items on top of the larger clothing items in the open area at the bottom.

The footlocker was also going to serve as our chair, desk, and work bench. We were never allowed to sit on our racks. The only time our butt hit the rack was when taps were called, and we were told to "hit the racks". All the rest of the time we had to sit on our footlocker. About the only time we even had time to sit on our footlocker was when we got "free time", which was given one hour before taps. Free time was for us to write letters home, shine our boots, polish our brass belt buckle, clean our rifles, and for just about any other thing we needed to work on. Our footlocker became our desk to write the letters home. It was our work bench for cleaning our rifle.

Sitting on a footlocker was not exactly the best seating we had had in our lives. The footlockers were wooden, and they offered no back-rest to lean back on. But, to us, having been standing on our feet all day, marching on the Grinder for hours, and running up to three miles, the footlocker was one of the sweetest places to put our butts. It gave our throbbing feet a moment of rest.

We were often required to bring the footlockers outside the Quonset huts, and line them up in two rows along the paved roadway in front of the huts. The drill instructor would call out: "*On the road with footlockers in 30 seconds!*" That meant that we had exactly 30 seconds to stop what we were doing, secure the footlockers, and pick them up, and be on the roadway within 30 seconds. On top of that, we had to repeat the drill instructors orders, starting at the first Quonset hut, and working down to the last: "Sir, on the road with foot lockers in 30 seconds, aye-aye sir!" In reality, the first Quonset hut (which was always the first squad) often was not prepared for the order, and was weak in their verbal response volume. The second, third and fourth squads would be louder as they got toward the end. There would be a mad dash with lots of commotion, and a lot of dust, while we ran to get the footlockers on the road within the 30 seconds. We never could.

"*I couldn't hear you! Get back inside your huts. Now!*" the DI would command. "Sir, aye-aye sir!" we would reply in unison and then we would scramble back inside with our footlockers in hand.

Once again, the DI would order: "On the road with footlockers in 30 seconds!" This time we were more prepared: "Sir, on the road with footlockers in 30 seconds, aye-aye sir!" Again, the command had to be repeated by each squad. Another mad dash was made to get outside within 30 seconds. Once again, not good enough for the DI: "*You ladies are taking too much time. You must want to play little girls' games with me. Get back inside your huts. Move it!*" The footlocker drill would continue for several more rounds before we finally sounded loud enough, and acted fast enough, to appease the DI. However, by that time we had carried a heavy wooden footlocker, laden with all our gear, back and forth, maybe five, or six times. We were totally exhausted by that point. We would then be given an instruction to clean rifles, or some other task that may have been needed.

The footlockers were required to be locked at all times. Failure to keep a footlocker locked was a significant failure to follow orders. Every now and then, a DI would come across an unlocked footlocker in the Quonset hut. He would open the locker, dump the contents on the deck, and kick the contents to scatter them. The drill instructor would yell: "*Why is this footlocker unlocked, Numb Nuts?*" The recruit would usually reply: "Sir, the private doesn't know, sir." At that point the drill instructor would say: "*Maggot-breath—you've got two minutes to get this garbage off my deck and get it back into the footlocker squared away. Once you have done that, report to the Duty Hut. Do you understand me?*"

"Sir, yes sir" he would reply. Once he reported he would be given incentive PT in the Pit as a reprimand.

The footlockers also were used in the evening just prior to us having taps, for what was known as "hygiene inspection". Hygiene inspection was a requirement of the DI's to ensure that we were both clean, and had no obvious physical problems with our feet, etc. About fifteen minutes before taps the DI would holler: "*Stand by for hygiene inspection.*" Each squad would successively repeat the command: "Sir, stand by for hygiene inspection, aye-aye, sir." We would then all grab our footlockers and line them up in two rows in the center of the hut, and then stand on top of them while wearing our skivvies, standing at the position of attention. The drill instructor would walk down each row and inspect us to ensure that our skivvies were clean, and to look at our feet to make sure they did not have any blisters. If there were any blisters or sores on anybodies feet, or any apparent medical issues, the recruit would be told to report to the DI in the morning to be sent to sick bay for treatment. It was extremely important that all the recruits were in good health. Once the hygiene inspection was over, the DI would command to the Quonset hut: "*Lights out, hatches closed, hit the racks!*" We would repeat the command as the drill instructor left to go to the next hut. Once the recruits were in their racks, they would all say in unison: "Good night Chesty Puller, where ever you are!"

On some occasions a DI would inspect a recruit's footlocker and ask: "Where the hell are you hiding the stick, private?" Confused, the private would reply: "Sir, the private does not know what stick the drill instructor is referring to, sir." The drill instructor would yell back: "*The stick you used to stir this shit up with in your footlocker, Numb Nut Breath! Get in the Pit and do push-ups until the ambulance comes!*"

THE FIELD DAY

Once each week we had to super-clean the Quonset huts or barracks. The process was referred to as a "field day". Cleaning the living quarters was more than just a dusting, and neatening process—it required scrubbing everything from the decks to the tops of the bulkheads, and everything in between. Boot camp environment created lots of dust, and the dust could settle into the smallest of crevices. There would be an inspection immediately after the field day, so everything had to be perfect.

We were assigned to specific cleaning tasks such as the urinals, the commodes, swabbing the decks, cleaning windows, etc. The squad leaders of each squad, as well as the platoon guide, were in charge of the process. If there could be such a thing as having a more or less desirable duty, cleaning the commodes and urinals ranked on the lowest spectrum of the pecking order.

Those assigned to the head detail always had to keep one commode and one urinal open for usage during the cleaning process. We had to be able to relieve ourselves if needed. The first order to cleaning was to clean the bulkheads first, going from top to bottom. Mirrors had to be polished clean. Sinks and the faucets had to be cleaned with a heavy scouring powder, and a scrub brush. All metal fittings were polished with a metal polish. The commodes and urinals were cleaned using the same cleaning agents. Once everything was scrubbed clean, and rinsed off, they then had to be wiped off so that there was no remaining water residue, or spots. When the upper areas were cleaned, then the process began on the decks. We would use the swabs (mops), and would first swab the decks with hot soapy water, then go back with hot clear water to pick up the soapy residue. The swabs had to be rinsed out continuously, and then wrung out over, and over, as the process progressed. There could be no marks left on the floor, including swabbing marks. Once the decks of the head were fully cleaned, the detail assigned would put a final touch on the commode bases that were impacted by the swabs. Then they would get on their hands and knees and wipe the decks with dry towels to remove any possible marks and streaks. The final commode and urinal would then be cleaned and the heads were closed until the inspection.

Cleaning the squad bays also required that the process start at the bulkheads and windows first. The bulkheads would be rubbed down with damp cloths from the ceiling down to the decks to remove dust and grime that had built up in the previous week. If we were in a barracks the window cleaners were assigned to clean both the inside and outside of the windows (unless we were in a barracks on the second floor). The heaters inside the Quonset huts were old-fashioned, oil burning heaters. Their usage would create a dark grimy substance inside of it, as well as in the exhaust pipes. These had to be cleaned with particular care, as it was the easiest thing for an inspecting drill instructor to determine was not fully cleaned.

The squad bay decks were the last to be cleaned. First, all the racks had to be moved over to one side of the area so that the floor could be completely cleaned on that side. Recruits would first sweep the deck (this sometimes created a cloud of dust that would land on the bulk heads and created a new cleaning issue) on the exposed open side. Then the swabbers would swab the decks with hot soapy water. That would be followed by swabbers using clean swabs, and hot water, to remove the water left by the first swabbers, and their soapy water. It was critical that the we had to get the decks very clean. Once the floors had the final swabbing, a crew of us would get on our hands and knees, and start at one end of the deck, wiping the deck with our towels to get a clean, and even surface without any marks. Once done with the deck on the one side, the racks would then be moved to the first side, and the process would be repeated on the second side. When we were all done we would put the racks in their appropriate spots. That last process could create marks on the decks so all of us would get on our hands and knees at one end of the squad bay, and start wiping the deck one last time with our cleaning towels. The final touch would be a group of us taking the brooms and we attached cleaning towels to the brooms' surfaces, and then went from one end of the squad bay to the other to get the final polishing touch to the decks. At that point no recruit was allowed on the deck surface, and those that were there doing the final touches had to be wearing only their socks to avoid marking the deck.

Every barracks and Quonset hut had several fifty gallon barrels used for trash. These barrels were made of galvanized steel. Each barrel was polished daily by one of us who used his brass cleaner to get the barrel to a highly polished sheen. During the field day these barrels had to be made spick and span like everything else. We took the barrels outside to make way for the other recruits assigned to cleaning the inside of the quarters. When we were done, the barrels were shiny like a new dime.

No matter what the procedure was, there was always someone that did not follow them. It always seemed like some recruit would sneak into the heads after everything was clean, and awaiting inspection, and use the commode or urinal. That always caused a last-minute rush to clean the soiled areas, and remove the footprints on the deck, and the other tell-tale signs of usage.

When everything was done, our squad leaders and our platoon guide would double-check, the triple-check everything to make sure the job was perfect Once they were satisfied they would notify the drill instructor in the duty office, and the DI would then come out to inspect our job.

"What's this?" the DI would ask, having run his hand along some obscure part of the bulkhead, and coming up with a little dust on his finger tips. *"You girls call this clean? Look at that deck—I can see streaking on it!"* He would walk over to the oil-burning heater, and put his hand inside the burner area—he always came up with coal-like blackness on his finger tips: *"This place is a sty! Everyone outside and get in the Pit!"*

After a thorough round of incentive training, to the point that we were totally exhausted, we would be ordered back inside the squad bay. There our drill instructor would go to random racks, and point out the numerous Irish Penants (loose material from the sheets and blankets hanging down under the spring supports). *"This is totally unacceptable ladies!"* After pushing over a couple of racks onto the deck he would order all the recruits to get out their scrub brushes, and line up on their hands and knees at one end of the squad bay deck, and he would make us start scrubbing with a dry brush going all the way to the other end. In some cases he would order us to use a tooth brush (one that was used for cleaning rifles) to scrub the area down. That would continue until the drill instructor was satisfied that we had done a good enough job.

Field days were not something that we looked forward to. The upside of the drill was that we were taught the importance of cleanliness, and how important that was in the Marine Corps. We all shared in the duties, so all of us had an experience cleaning commodes, urinals, and all the other dirty jobs we never had to do at home. From that point going forward, we would be always be able to thoroughly clean our quarters, and would take a pride in keeping them clean. Marines live clean.

One thing that we quickly learned about the field days: the drill instructor was *never* going to be satisfied. The DI could always find something that we had overlooked.

HAND-TO-HAND COMBAT

For me, one of the most hard-core lessons about what being a Marine was all about came to me during the Close Combat training. For some reason I had always perceived combat to be just a long distance affair in which the enemy was a distance away, and there would be a barrier of space between the enemy and me. That perception would change in a big way when I stepped onto the Close Combat training course for our first lesson.

It was here that we were taught that sometime it might be necessary to fight so close to the enemy that we would have to engage in hand-to-hand fighting. Close combat training was going to prepare us to use our rifles, bayonets, hands, and even our teeth if needed, to engage the enemy at close quarters. The instructors were all very experienced in that subject. One of the instructors was Staff Sergeant Bill Paxton who was partly responsible for that training syllabus coming about. I would meet up with him over twenty years later in the Marine Corps Drill Instructors Association—I discovered later that he would be one of the most storied and colorful Marines I would ever meet.

The first rule we were to learn about hand-to-hand combat was: *there were no rules*. Hand-to-hand combat "was up-close and personal fighting". The winner lived, and the loser *died*. We were told to throw out all previous ideas of "fairness" about fighting. When engaged, it would be a fight to the death, and we were expected to do whatever it took to take out the enemy. That might include gouging an eye out or biting off a nose. We would learn that our bodies were weapons, and the training would teach us how to use our bodies and equipment to *kill the enemy*.

"Kill the enemy." That thought really hit me during that phase of training. Up to that point, training had seemed just sort of "military". Suddenly it was sinking in that we were being trained to *kill*. That was the whole point of Close Combat Training. Learning to kill was not an every-day subject that you found in the library. The instructors were going to make it very clear that we would be fully trained, and capable of completing that mission should the occasion arise.

The use of a knife or bayonet was the first order of training. The instructors informed us how to lunge, slash, and jab the weapons for effective kills. We had to practice various movements using a piece of rubber hose that was about eighteen inches long to simulate a knife or bayonet. Recruits would be paired up, and would go through various combative movements against one another. Over and over, we repeated each deadly blow, or motion. They continuously talked about the purpose of the fight was to take out the enemy: in other words, *to eliminate him*. The fairness aspect of fighting we all came to boot camp with was quickly being wiped out of our minds. Combat fighting has no fairness. The enemy can't be just "winged": he must be taken out completely to eliminate him as a threat to ourselves, and our units.

Choking an enemy to death was another option that was taught. We were to find out that a person can be dead in as few as ten seconds with the proper choke technique. We were not just instructed about this, but we had to perform it on our assigned partners. It did not take more than one run through to discover that the choker has the better side of it than the person being choked! When being choked, you could actually feel the life slowly going out of you as the oxygen and blood flow to the brain was being deprived. That was actually very dangerous training—the instructors were teaching over 350 recruits in a fairly large area. It was possible for a problem to arise before the instructor could intervene. There were a few recruits that we choked for longer than consciousness was possible, and they had to be revived. But, despite the dangers, it was vital training and had to be taught.

We were also instructed about basic judo movements to teach us how to throw the enemy down, or to repel the enemy if we were attacked. It always boiled down to the basic human survival instincts. We had to practice these movements again, and again, so that they would be second nature to us. They taught us that there was always the possibility that we could face an enemy with no weapon at all. That was when we learned about using our teeth to bite anything, and everything we could, to take out the enemy. Tearing off an ear, or gouging an eye out with a finger, was presented to us as though we were being taught how to clean an M-14. After a while the aspect of killing another person just becomes part of the process: it no longer came to us as a chilling thought. This part of the training made me realize that we were being trained to be *killers*.

The use of a rifle as a weapon seemed obvious, but more than a shooting instrument, it also was an effective club. With a bayonet attached, it also could be used as a sword-like weapon. In close combat situations the enemy may be too close to shoot the weapons, necessitating hand-to-hand techniques instead. Using the butt of the rifle stock as a club, the rifle could be swung around in a round-house hook, or an upward motion to hit the enemy on the head with a killing blow—if it didn't kill the enemy it would surely knock him unconscious. With the bayonet attached the weapon could be thrust forward to gorge the enemy, or to slash his throat in one swing. Using our rifles with bayonets attached (the bayonet scabbards were also on for safety-sake), we practiced the actual motions needed on those strokes. Repetition, after repetition, we practiced the teachings.

When the training was completed about how to use the weapons, we were then given a more practical lesson at the "Pugil Stick Course". Pugil sticks were poles roughly the length of an M-14 rifle, with heavy padding on both ends. There were padded glove handles in the middle of the pole for us to place our hands in to hold the pugil sticks like we might an M-14 rifle. We were issued a football helmet for head protection, and then paired off, with two recruits starting the bouts in a ring area about twenty feet in diameter. We would then attack each other, with the object to win the bout by delivering the first deadly blow to the opponent. The instructors were the judges. Each round went on until one of us delivered a killing blow. These pugil sticks were fairly heavy, and the bouts could be extremely tiring. We had to be aggressive or we faced the wrath of both the instructor, and our drill instructors. Everyone fought "to the death". That was not a time to be a wimp. Despite the heavy padding and the helmets, being hit with a butt-stroke on the head, or a lunging blow to the chest area, hurt! Every blow could be felt, not only at the time of the blow, but for a long time after in the form of aching muscles, headaches and more.

The pugil stick training would occur on many occasions since it was the best means of simulating combat. Eventually the instructors made a little fun out of it by having the best pugil stick fighters of each platoon in our series go against the other platoons' best fighters. That created a lot of team spirit and made for a good competition. I did fairly well for being one of the smaller men in my platoon, and in the inter-platoon competition I got down to the top five in my platoon by being able to come in lower and capitalize on getting rapid killer blows. Unfortunately for me, I got my clock rung my last time out. I was "killed".

Despite the realization that we were there being trained to kill, that was a very memorable part of boot camp. We got to work off a lot of aggression during those sessions. To this day I believe that *any* Marine would be a major threat in a fight due to that training, and their understanding that there are no rules in fighting. *You win, you live. You lose, you die.*

IT SEEMED LIKE FOREVER

For most recruits, boot camp seemed like a surreal event. It continued to unroll like a bad dream. The drill instructors were on us constantly, never letting up, and never letting anything get by them. We had been separated from those we loved, and we had only other recruits to draw support from. In looking back, it makes sense now—the Marines in combat situations are in the same position, as they too must rely on their combat buddies for support. We definitely were not going to be getting it from Mom!

One of the disheartening revelations in boot camp was when we discovered that the Processing Phase was not part of the training cycle. That phase was a killer, as it was when the drill instructors really laid into us to set the tone for the training ahead. The DI's yelled constantly. Nothing we did was fast enough, loud enough, or good enough. We had to repeat everything over, and over. We were learning new things very quickly, and at the same time we had to forget many of the things we had grown up to believe to be the way to do things.

Each day was filled with tough issues from the moment we woke in the mornings, till we finally were allowed to hit the racks at night. We were required to memorize our new service numbers, rifle numbers, and other details that we had to recall on demand. Forty years after boot camp I can still rattle off my service number without hesitation.

First Phase was filled with drill, classroom lessons, and military indoctrination. As First Phase recruits, we looked very horrible as far as Marine Corps standards go. By design, our uniforms were worn in such a manner as to identify us as First Phase recruits. We could not blouse the trouser legs around our boots (tucking them inward and securing them by an elastic cord), so the trouser legs hung too long, and draped over the boot tops. We also had to button the top button on our utility blouses. Our covers were not starched and shaped yet, so they too were a dead giveaway of our status. Plus, we had that pale look that only a new recruit had once his hair had been shaved off. As if the uniform and haircuts were not enough of a giveaway, we just looked, and acted sloppy all the time!

Our initiation to marching was to a very slow cadence (marching speed). It was so slow that it was comical to watch. Instead of marching at the normal cadence of 120 steps per minute we were marching at maybe forty steps per minute. Even then, there were recruits that could not keep it together with the rest of the platoon. Our sloppiness would cause many repetitions of bends and thrusts when the DI's wanted to "tighten us up." Our drill with the rifle movements, called rifle manual of arms, was also comical. Not being used to the manual of arms drill, we were very jerky in our movements, and we constantly were moving our heads to prevent the weapons from hitting us on the noggins. Of course that was caught by the ever-vigilant drill instructors and more incentive physical training (PT) would ensue, often doing rifle incentive PT, which involved many repetitions of lifting the rifle over our heads till our arms could no longer hold the rifles up. Each day we got better though. Toward the end of First Phase we actually looked fairly good at marching and rifle manual, but the cadence was still very slow.

Physical training (PT) was another new ordeal for most recruits. During that era kids in junior and senior high school had to take gym classes in an effort to get physically fit. That stemmed from President Kennedy's' fitness program. However, having an hour of gym class each day did not prepare one for Marine Corps boot camp—it was not even close! We were immediately introduced to push ups, bends and thrusts, jumping-jacks, sit-ups and other exercises almost as soon as we got to our Quonset huts on our first night. Each morning, just after reveille, we had to go out and do "wake-up" exercises before we could go to the mess hall. Later in the day we had physical training (PT) out on the PT field. PT lasted about an hour, but it seemed more like three hours by the time we were done. We also had to do a platoon run each day. Initially the runs started with one mile, and then increased to two miles within about a week or so. By the time First Phase was ending we were running three miles. Runs during the Vietnam era were done in combat boots to simulate running in combat.

The chow (food) was another thing we had to get used to. It certainly was not like home cooking. But it did not take long for us to realize that we were burning calories by the thousands due to all the activities we had to endure each day. The chow started to get better and better as far as we were concerned. We could not seem to get enough of it, either. I found that there were recruits in my platoon that were willing to pay cash money for an extra piece of cake: I made a few extra bucks selling my deserts to them. We were allowed to take all the chow we wanted, but had to eat everything on the trays. I do not recall anybody going back a second time as it also required getting the drill instructors' permission, and the hassle of doing that was too much to bear.

By the end of First Phase we were allowed to blouse our trousers around our boots. That gave us a more Marine-like appearance and we started to feel like we were making some progress. That also meant that we were going to the rifle range to learn how to shoot the rifles. We did not know what to expect, but it sounded better than what we had been going through.

Second Phase took place at the rifle range at Edson Range in Camp Pendleton, California, about 45 minutes north on Interstate 5. Upon our arrival there, my platoon realized we were very lucky because we were being assigned to a barracks instead of tents in the "Tent City" alongside the freeway. Tent City was an area consisting of tents that housed about six to eight recruits each. They were cold, windy, and existence there would have been terrible conditions to endure on top of everything else. We also learned that the first week there we were assigned to "mess week" and we were going to be doing mess-duty for seven straight days. Mess duty was a very grueling and tedious task that required recruits to stand on their feet all day. The mess week day goes from about 0330 until after 2130 at night (3:30 AM to 9:30 PM). There was very little time for sleep, and virtually no free time to write letters home. When mess week ended it was truly something to rejoice about. I was extremely lucky in that I was assigned with four other recruits to mess duty at the Staff NCO Club. We helped serving the meals, cleaning the pots and pans, and sweeping and polishing the floors twice per day. Although it was long and tedious work, we ate better than the other recruits because we ate the same food that was served to the Staff NCOs, and we had shorter hours because the club did not open till later in the morning than the mess hall, and it closed earlier in the evening. We were also treated pretty well by the staff and patrons of the club. However, I was glad when it was over so we could get down to the task of rifle training.

The rifle we would be qualifying with was the M-14 rifle. It weighed about 9 ½ pounds. The instructors that taught the classes were called Preliminary Marksmanship Instructors (PMI's). The first week we were taught how the sights worked, and how to squeeze the triggers. We spent most of the day dry-shooting by doing what is referred to as "snapping-in". Snapping-in meant that we were aiming the rifles at miniature targets and squeezing the triggers. It was part of the process of learning that, in order to hit the target successfully, the trigger had to be squeezed, not jerked. Many hours were spent on the ground, imitating shooting. We could not wait for the real shooting to begin. We also got to shoot the .45 caliber automatic pistol at one of the pistol ranges. Most of us would not ultimately have to qualify with the pistol, as that was determined by the military occupational specialty (MOS) we would be assigned by the time we graduated. It was primarily to acquaint us with the pistol so we had a rudimentary understanding of how it functioned should the need ever arise to have to use one in a combat situation.

Our drill instructors used the evening hours, while at the rifle range, to teach more drill movements we would need to learn for the Final Drill Evaluation in Third Phase. They also took us on long runs, and made sure that we still did the PT needed to remain in shape for the Physical Fitness Test we would also have when we returned to MCRD, San Diego. They were really tough on us during Snapping-in Week. That would change dramatically during qualifying week, as they suddenly stopped being so hard on us, and actually lightened-up. During that week there was very little incentive PT training as the week progressed. The DI's would talk to us in the evenings about their experiences in the Marine Corps in order to create a more relaxed atmosphere.

The final week at the rifle range was the week of qualifying. The first four days were for getting used to firing the high powered, 7.62 mm rifles. The sights had to be properly set up on each recruits' rifle. Friday of that week was qualifying day. It was really tough on everyone because we *had to qualify* to proceed to Third Phase. In order to qualify, a recruit had to shoot a minimum of 190 points out of a possible 250 points. Thursday was pre-qualification (prequal day) day and the recruits went through a complete qualification drill. If in the unlikely event that weather would not permit shooting on Friday, the pre-qualification scores could be used. On Prequal Day I was the range high-shooter with a score of 242. That night my DI paraded me in front of the platoon, and raved over my performance. I felt really good about things, and it was a high-point for me up to that time. When Friday came, things would be different. On that day fog had settled in during the night before, and the sky was dark and gloomy. Our sights had been set up for sunny conditions and all the settings would be off. In my case, my qualifying score dropped down to 195, and I barely qualified. I was terribly disappointed in my low score, even though I qualified. My drill instructor was also disappointed in my low score, and I had to spend time in the Pit to pay penance for my poor shooting after such a high score the day before. At least I qualified! That also allowed me to make a ten minute phone call home when we were to return on Saturday. Despite my poor showing, my platoon actually had the highest qualifying scores out of our four-platoon series, and we ended up with the series ribbon for our superior shooting. The ribbon would be proudly placed on the platoon Gideon, which was the platoon flag on a large staff, held by the Platoon Guide in the front of the platoon. We were elated.

We returned to San Diego the next day, and began Third Phase. One of the benefits of that phase was being allowed to unbutton the top button of our utility blouse. We were starting to look like real Marines. The end was getting near, and we were taking on a serious team pride about our platoon. However, the drill instructors suddenly reverted to their in your face tactics, and we just could not seem to do anything right again. We started to spend a lot more time in the Pit.

My platoon took the Final Drill Evaluation honors and we received the ribbon for that. Our Gideon now had the two best honors: the Rifle Range ribbon and the Final Drill ribbon. We felt pretty good about our accomplishment as a platoon and it was a tribute to our DI's that we were the best.

During boot camp I wrote home to my wife every night. Sometimes there was insufficient time during free-time with all the preparations that were necessary, so I often wrote the letters using a flashlight under my blanket after taps. If I had been caught by my DI or the Officer-of-the-Day I would have been punished, but it was important to me to communicate to her. I never got caught. One of my high points of Third Phase was getting to call home as a reward for qualifying with the rifle. It was hard to describe how good a loved one's voice sounded when you haven't spoken to them for a while. For ten minutes I was away from boot camp and back into my real world—it was really great!

We had to get our full issue of uniforms before we graduated. There would be a final inspection of all that gear in what was known as a "junk-on-the-bunk" inspection—all the gear was laid out on the rack and it had to be properly stamped with our names, all in very precise and neat order. In addition we had to stand the Final Inspection in our dress uniforms to make sure that the uniforms fit properly. During the Final Inspection we had to be able to answer questions about Marine Corps history, our general orders, and other things that the inspector felt like asking. My platoon passed this inspection with flying colors.

In looking back on my experiences with the DI's I can honestly say that there were times when I absolutely hated them. From my very first experience, when I could not get words to come out of my mouth, until graduation, the experience was primarily one of fear and hate. During each phase of training we had felt that the DI's were mean, sadistic bullies, hell-bent on making our lives as miserable as they could. However, in the end we all ended up with the absolute highest respect and regard for them. They had pushed us to the edge, and many times pushed us *over* the edge. In the end we had endured their wrath and we came away stronger than we could have ever believed was possible. Our drill instructors became etched in our minds forever. Every boot camp moment, no matter how harsh, would remain with us. The DI's set a standard for our lives that remains to this day. They had made us into United States Marines.

AGAINST ALL ODDS

My original goal in joining the Marine Corps was to evade the draft. I was totally opposed to the Vietnam War and had no interest in participating directly in it, but first, and foremost, I did not want to be drafted into the Army. To me, that would have been the ultimate take-away of my individual freedom, specifically, the freedom of choice. The draft was very unpopular, and many chose to evade it by not registering with the Selective Service, not showing up when drafted, or simply fleeing to Canada. All of those choices were illegal, and were signs of cowardice in my mind. I rationalized that opposing the war was not a good enough reason to not serve your country, so serving was not out of the question to me.

When I first spoke to my recruiter, I told him of my desire to be in the administrative side of the Marines, and of my desire to not go to Vietnam. He quickly informed me that the Marine Corps existed to fight wars, and that all Marines went to Vietnam, and with only the two year enlistment that I was willing to sign up for, he could not guarantee me a specific billet. I would be subject to the whims of the Marine Corps needs. Despite his honesty, I still chose to opt for the two year enlistment, and take my chances.

By the time I had completed boot camp I was a changed person, as everyone who has experienced Marine Corps boot camp will claim. On the last day of boot camp the Platoon Commander sat down with the platoon, and he gave everyone their military occupational specialty (MOS), along with their first set of orders. One by one he called out the recruits in alphabetical order, and gave them their MOS, and duty assignments. Most were going to be 0311, which meant infantry, and all had orders to WestPac which stood for Western Pacific, and was tantamount to saying "Vietnam". Some were going to be cooks, some truck drivers, others the Air Wing specialties. But all were given WestPac orders. Finally he came to me—"Private Stoner—you are going to be a 0141 which means you are going to be a clerk typist admin-man, and you are going to Parris Island, South Carolina." I was stunned by the good news—I was reaching the goal I had set off to achieve—administration duties and no Vietnam! This was almost too good to be true. The really ironic thing was that I was the only one of the 85 recruits in my platoon to remain stateside—all the rest were issued orders to WestPac.

All recruits during this era were sent to infantry training at Camp Pendleton upon graduation from boot camp. All Marines are first, and foremost, rifleman, and infantry training was something that every Marine must learn no matter what MOS they have. The morning after graduation we said our goodbyes to our drill instructors, and boarded busses for the trip up to Camp Pendleton, to begin our infantry training phase.

Before training began, we were all assigned to either maintenance duty, or guard duty for one week. My assignment was guard duty, and I got my first taste of a more typical Marine setting than the boot camp environment I had lived with for the past three months. Guard duty was strenuous—four hours on, four hours off. This continued twenty-four hours per day for a week. My duty assignment was to guard the armory. One would think that an armory at a Marine Corps base would be fairly secure, but the fact was, it was a potential target by radical groups due to its supply of weapons. The Corporal-of-the-Guard made it abundantly clear that the reason we were issued live ammunition for our M-14 rifles was that we may need to use it. While this was a far cry from the dangers of Vietnam, I was acutely aware of the potential of lurking danger in every shadow and movement around the perimeter of the armory. It really started to dawn on me what the Marines do. I was very glad when the guard duty ended and training began. At least I thought I was glad.

We were assigned to training companies and we had "troop handlers" in charge of us instead of drill instructors. Most of the troop handlers were either corporals or sergeants, and most had recently returned from Vietnam duty. They were nowhere near the caliber of NCO that our drill instructors had been. The atmosphere at Infantry Training was not nearly as strict as boot camp. The troop handlers could best be described as "wanna-be drill instructors", and we all felt it was best to avoid direct contact with them if that was possible.

Infantry training in the Marines took place out in the field. That meant "*way out*". The way we got way out in the field was on foot. That was to be my first experience with "route step march" which was a form of marching, but not staying in step as the platoons in the company were traveling on very uneven ground. They also seemed to travel at different speeds—the platoon in the front set the pace and the platoons following needed to keep up. That sometimes meant running. The company tended to "accordion" during the marches—the rear platoon always struggling to keep up with the front platoon. Camp Pendleton is on the coast of

California, and is comprised of coastal foothills that rise to 1500 foot elevations or more. Most of the training locations took place in areas somewhere up in the mountains and foot hills. Platoons rout-stepped up the hillsides, at what to the marchers, seemed to be straight up. My platoon was the last one in the company so we had to run more then rest. That was in hot August days with temperatures hovering in the nineties.

Rout-stepping up the side of a mountain on a hot August day with a full pack on your back, and an M-14 rifle in your arms, was not an easy task. In fact, it felt more like *torture*. I vividly recall one hill that we were climbing at a full gallop that just sucked the desire to proceed right out of me. I was using my last possible iota of strength, and inner fortitude, to try and make the peak, but was losing the cause, along with many others. I finally had to just drop to the ground, out of breath, and out of any energy, or desire to continue. Suddenly I felt the neck of my blouse pull tight, and I heard PFC Hutchinson yell to me: "*Get going Pvt Stoner—you can't give up now!*" Here was my bunk-mate goading me on. All at once I realized that Marines do not give up; that we just had to keep going, so I climbed to my feet, and continued on, with an inner drive that I did not know existed previously. PFC Hutchinson taught me a lesson that lives with me to this day. Marines *never give up—ever*.

The marches were the hardest part of the whole time at infantry training. The actual training was a piece-of-cake. Training usually consisted of shooting specific weapons like the M-60 machine gun, throwing grenades, shooting a bazooka, etc. We also learned how to read a compass, read topography maps, how to identify tunnels, trip wires, and other need-to-know things. Most of the lessons were about really neat things for guys and we all loved it.

Often the company would be out in the field on a training mission for twenty-four hours or more. We spent the night in the field on some occasions, and ate C-rations. On some jaunts we marched all through the day so that we could do a live-fire maneuver that night. Night shooting exercises were pretty scary—it was totally dark out in the foothills, and we were shooting live rounds. Tracers were going everywhere. Rifle bursts filling the air with a frightening roar. People were moving around and rotating positions—all in pitch darkness. After the exercises were over we would start our return to the barracks. The return march was also very frightening. We were often running at a full run, down trails that were very uneven, full of ruts, rocks and obstacles. One wrong placement of a foot and it would be over for that person if his boot caught a rut. Rattle snakes were also very prevalent to the area. To this day, I am amazed that we did not lose more Marines doing these night maneuvers. I for one, felt very lucky that I did not break a leg or ankle during the process.

Our uniforms were totally saturated in sweat almost all of the time. When we got back to the barracks we would hang our saturated uniforms in our lockers, and then put on our previous day's uniform which was still damp. This went on day after day. Our socks were able to dry out during the night as we placed them over our racks, and there was sufficient air to dry them before reveille in the mornings. Reveille came early too—0500 (5:30 AM) no matter when we got in the night before. We would rush off to the mess hall where we ate as many calories as we could consume to prepare for the schedule for that day. We knew that every single calorie was going to get burned off before the next breakfast.

The Troop Handlers at infantry training were all veteran Marines that had returned from Vietnam duty. Some were going to be career Marines, but many were just waiting the end of their enlistments. Unfortunately for us, they tried to be like DI's and were very harsh on us. If they felt we needed to be "tightened up" they would issue incentive PT training that was a lot different than what we had in boot camp. One of the exercises they gave us was called "dying cockroach". It required that we lie on the ground and extend our arms and legs straight up, shaking the legs and arms like a cockroach on his back, dying. After a few moments of this the entire body and torso felt like it was exploding. Another of their favorite sessions was to have us "duck-walk". To duck-walk it was necessary to crouch down with knees bent, and the buttocks close to the ground, and then walking forward in that position. The motion it made looked like a duck walking. The exercise put an extreme strain on the thigh muscles that would result in extreme cramps. On one occasion I experienced a totally senseless act of brutality: I was in the head at a urinal when a sergeant came in, and walked up to a nearby urinal. He started talking—I did not see anyone else in the head and I assumed he was talking to me, so I answered whatever he was asking. He turned to me, grabbed me by my blouse and shoved me up against a bulkhead, and said "What in the hell are you talking to me for, Asshole? Did you think I was talking to you?" He then drew back and hit me in the stomach as hard as he could. He thought he was tough, but in my eyes I saw a person who totally lacked any leadership ability. I have never forgotten his senseless brutality.

The single worst experience in infantry training was the gas chamber. There is nothing on this planet that can prepare anyone for this experience. Once again we had to route-step march to the gas chamber which was somewhere way off in the valleys far from base camp. The heat of the day made for heavy sweat, and coupled with the fact that our utility uniforms were already wet, we were uncomfortable all of the time. The chamber was a Quonset hut in the middle of a clearing. We were all issued a gas mask, and went through a very thorough training on how to put it on, adjust it, and ensure that it was working properly. We all thought that the drill would be to make sure that the masks worked when we went inside the chamber. We were then given a lecture on what exactly the tear gas was, and how it worked, and some of its dangers. Emphasis was on making sure that we knew how to properly place the masks on once gas was detected. More practice. We were finally ordered to don the masks, and one squad at a time was sent into the gas chamber. Inside the squad was put into two rows facing one another. In the middle of the hut was a canister that the instructor was putting something into that was making gaseous fumes. There were maybe a half dozen instructors or aides in the hut as well. The instructor told the group opposite my side to remove their masks, and to start singing the Marine Corps Hymn. They removed their masks, and began singing. It looked mild at first, and I was beginning to think this was going to be sort of easy. But the Marines had to breathe in at some point, and a few lines into the hymn they all started to breathe in for air—only there *was no air*, only the gas rising constantly from the canister. Their faces contorted, and they all immediately began to cough, and gasp, and a look of terror came over their faces. Every opening on their faces was drooling slobber or snot. Their eyes were running, and they were all looking like death would have been a welcomed event. It seemed like the instructors kept them there with their masks off for an eternity—it seemed very sadistic to me. One at a time they were given the okay to put their masks on, clear them, and then were allowed to exit the hut. Each man wildly ran toward the hatch, and lunged outside to take in fresh air, fluids continuing to drain from all their body openings. It was not a pretty site.

Then it was our turn. The instructor put more stuff in the canister. I was beginning to wish that I had been the first group who were caught by surprise— my group now knew full well what to expect, and it was not something we were looking forward to. We all had the same strategy in our minds—hold our breaths, and sing the hymn, and be done with it in short order. Right! With gas emanating from the canister, we were ordered to remove the gas masks, and begin singing the Marines Hymn. Quickly the masks were removed and a rapidly sung hymn began to chime out—"From the halls of ..." *Bam!* The gas hit like being kicked in the groin. Our reaction began with a cough, and then a gasp, and then it started to permeate everywhere in our bodies. I can best describe it by saying our insides wanted to turn to our outsides. The body convulsed in revulsion of the gas. Snot flowed like a river from our noses. Slobber came out of our mouths like the green stuff that came out of the mouth of the girl in the movie the "Exorcist." Every square inch of our exposed skin was burning. Our lungs were exploding—and every explosion took in a new breath of fresh tear gas, making it even worse. Death soon became a desire to end it all. Surviving this was now our first priority—we felt like we were going to die, and actually would have looked forward to it, when finally, the trainers told us to put our gas masks on, and clear the masks. Once done we could leave. We lunged outside through the hatches. Outside we pulled our masks off, and gasped for air. The affects of tear gas do not leave immediately—it takes more than a few moments to finally get a handle on it. In the meantime, all the other Marines that hadn't gone in yet were looking at the results, and you could see the fear in their eyes. We were all lying on the ground trying to recover from our horrible experience. I made a vow to myself that I never, ever, wanted to go through anything like that again—a vow that I did not know I would not be able to keep. To this day I can acutely spot the aroma of CS tear-gas in a New York heartbeat.

Infantry training did have some high points. Since that was war-time, we were treated to a USO show to bring up morale. Having seen these shows in movies, and knowing that the likes of Bob Hope made the tours, the show was a special treat for the Marines at Camp Pendleton. I can see how the troops in faraway places would get a big morale boost out of these shows—it was extremely uplifting to those of us that were undergoing training. There were bands, dancing girls, and comedians to make us laugh. I realized the value of these shows and I applaud all those volunteers that were involved.

The biggest highlight of my infantry training was a weekend of off-base liberty. This was the first time I could travel home, and see my newlywed wife Melody, since before I had left for boot camp. It was the happiest weekend I had in over four month's time. I relished every single minute of it, and absolutely hated to return on Sunday. Once again, I bid Melody goodbye, and went back for more training punishment.

I was glad I was not in the infantry because for those of us who weren't, our training only lasted two weeks—infantry Marines had to go on for another three weeks.

With the training completed for the non-infantry Marines we were able to take a leave, and go home for 10 days. Nothing seemed to feel as great as being able to go home, and erase the darkness that we had gone through from the past three to four months. Melody picked me up at our base camp, and I was able to return home for a brief honeymoon. I was a different man than when I had first entered. My body was much more toned, and I had lost a lot of weight. My muscles had become rock-hard. How good it felt to be away from the regimens we had been through, even though it was short lived.

Infantry training left its mark on me though—I ended up with a severe case of shin splints on both legs due to the constant pounding on the marches we had. It took all of my leave, and most of the subsequent four weeks of clerk school training, to heal from the ordeal.

When my leave was over I drove up the freeway from home, and I checked in to Clerk Typist School at Camp Pendleton, and for the first time since I had joined, I started to feel like a *real* Marine. No more troop handlers, DI's, or the like. We were on our own at last, and it was a pleasant relief. I was even able to commute daily from my home forty miles south. Clerk School was fairly easy too—mostly methods of keeping company records, and reporting daily staffing issues such as transfers. Lots of detailed stuff, and the kind of things I liked to deal with. I was a good typist, and typing played a large part of the process. This school lasted about 4 weeks, and once done, I was to journey to my first duty station at Parris Island, South Carolina. Since I was going to drive to my next duty station with my wife, I was given travel time as well. We had about two weeks to get to Parris Island. That would give us a little time off before we had to leave.

My wife and I packed our things, spent a few more days with our friends and relatives, and then headed east toward Parris Island, South Carolina. This was our first trip anywhere together, and my wife's first trip that far in a car. It took us about five days to complete the trip. We spent three days just getting through Texas alone. It was hard to realize just how large our nation was. We arrived at Beaufort, South Carolina, right in the midst of a hurricane approaching. I had never seen wind so powerful. We sat in our motel huddled in front of the TV watching the news, and wondering if we would survive the ordeal. Like all storms it finally quieted down, and things got back to normal.

On the Friday after arrival, I checked into Headquarters Company at Parris Island. I was interviewed by the company commander. He looked at my records, and quickly concluded that I had two and one-half years of college, and I was a rapid typist. He told me he was going to assign me to the Drill Instructor School to replace the chief clerk, who was being transferred to Vietnam. "Oh my God" I said to myself, "They are assigning me to where they train those bastards!" I was beginning to think I had gone from the pot to the skillet. I was to report to the Drill Instructor School on the following Monday.

Against all odds, my original goals were coming together.

CHECKING IN

When I first checked into Headquarters Company at Parris Island, and was told that my duty assignment was going to be to replace the Chief Clerk at the Drill Instructor School, my heart almost stopped. I immediately began to conger up thoughts of my recent drill instructor's yelling; screaming, and making recruits do things we never thought possible. Now I was going to be assigned to where they trained the drill instructors. My mind raced with what to expect.

My wife and I had moved into an old trailer in a small trailer park in Beaufort, South Carolina, when we first arrived. I told her of my assignment, and she too had reservations. All weekend long we thought about what to expect. Nothing in the training so far had prepared me for this assignment.

Finally, my day of reckoning came as Monday arrived. I put on my uniform, and set out for my first official Marine Corps duty assignment. I arrived with a lot of trepidation. With all the courage I could muster, I got out of my car, and proceeded toward the front doors of the one story building that had a big yellow sign with red letters that said: Drill Instructor School. Major Bruce, Director; 1stSgt Figueroa Chief NCOIC (Noncommissioned Officer In Charge). I walked up to the door, took my garrison cap off my head, and tucked it neatly under my belt to hold it in place like I had seen the other Marines do in Schools Battalion at Camp Pendleton. I walked into the building. I was immediately met by a tall, slender super squared-away Gunnery Sergeant by the name of Horton. In a very stern voice he asked what I was doing there. I began to envision boot camp all over. I mustered up the courage to say that I was checking in to become the clerk. He looked down at my garrison cap tucked in my belt, and in a firmer voice than earlier said *"PFC, if the Marine Corps had intended you to place your garrison cap in your belt they would have issued you a hook there—now get it out of there right now, and never put it there again!"* Welcome to the Drill Instructors School!

One of my first duty assignments at the school was to make coffee in a large 40 cup coffee urn in our coffee mess. I had never made coffee before, but after being shown how it was done, it didn't seem that hard. So the first time I made it

I decided I would speed the process up by putting *hot* water in the large pot. The water was extremely hot at Parris Island. I figured the less time the brewer took to heat the water; the faster the coffee would be available. I started to hear the instructors grumbling in the other room, and before long, one of them came into my office, and asked me if I had made the coffee yet. I told him I did much earlier. It was then that I found out that the thermostat for the brewer never triggered because the water was so hot. I had to make a new pot, and this delay did not hold me in high favor with the instructors. I never made that mistake again.

I was a PFC (Private First Class), and I was replacing a sergeant. The billet actually called for a sergeant, or staff sergeant, to handle the job. In addition to me, the school had Sergeant Cephus, who was our general maintenance person. There were approximately six or seven instructors at the school. The director of the school was Major Bruce, who was a bull of a man. He was the first officer I was ever around, and he scared me to death. First Sergeant Figueroa was the Chief Instructor at the school. All of the rest of the instructors were gunnery sergeants. They all were the top drill instructors at MCRD, Parris Island.

The Drill Instructor Schools are the premier schools of the Marine Corps, I was to learn. There was one at San Diego, and one at Parris Island. A lot of competition existed between the two for who was best. They attracted a lot of attention, and were often the first places that dignitaries were shown when visiting the bases. I was quickly learning of the significance of my new duty slot.

The students that were attending the school during the Vietnam era were primarily NCOs (noncommissioned officers) that were returning from duty in Vietnam. Even though the duty of being a drill instructor was considered one of the premier positions for a Marine to achieve, it was not something that every Marine wanted. Many of the Marines returning from Vietnam were shell-shocked veterans who had spent some harrowing time in Vietnam. Many had purple hearts for wounds in action. All were highly decorated. But there was an attitude among many candidates, that the job of drill instructor was potentially a career killer, because they had heard there was a high number of Marines that were relieved from duty for maltreatment of recruits, or violations of the SOP (Standard Operating Procedures). The hours of a drill instructor were extreme also, and many just wanted to spend as much time with their families as they could, without the added stresses the drill field brought with it.

The potential candidates went through a screening by the school instructors, and the director. The interviews were probing, and the board was looking for candidates that represented the true value of NCO leadership, and the qualities that a Marine drill instructor must possess to perpetuate the stellar image of the drill instructor and the Marine Corps. They wanted to screen out those candidates that were potentially prone to sadistic behavior with the potential to maltreat the recruits. The board would end up doing a silent vote right in front of the students: they did so by taking their pens or pencils, and either held it upright on the desk for a yes, or placed it flat on the desk for a no. The candidates were immediately advised they had either been voted into the school, or rejected. Somehow the candidates never caught on as to how the board had voted.

The school would start with about forty students. Through the process of the training they eventually would eliminate about one third to one half of the students for a variety of reasons. Some just did not have the leadership needed to be a DI. Some did not have the capacity to learn the many movements of drill, and other teaching techniques that were required to become a DI. Some just did not have the requisite physical capability to endure the extreme conditions of training recruits. The training of the DI's was extremely grueling, and required long hours of study, practicing presentations of drill movements, and being ready for the many inspections that were held. Drill Instructor School was another form of boot camp in reality. The only real difference between DI School training and recruit training was that the DI students were treated with the dignity, and respect of an NCO, and the students were able to go home every night. The rest was basically almost the same.

My job was to handle the student records, type the many letters and memos from the director, and to type reports submitted by the instructors regarding the students. I had to learn quickly. The person I replaced left for Vietnam about three weeks after I started, and I had only cursory training from him as to what I had to do. Basically, I had to learn on-the-job as it developed. It was kind of scary in that type of environment. I often had to decipher the many abbreviations and acronyms of students' prior commands when submitting the various documentations. I recall that I had to stay late one night, alone in the school, finishing up on some reports that had to get out. I was stuck on acronyms that made no sense to me. I did not know what to do. It was 2030 hours (8:30 PM), and there was nobody present at the school to ask. It occurred to me to call the one person that I felt might have some answers for me: the Officer-of-the-Day for the Depot. I explained my predicament, and he gladly assisted me in deciphering the acronyms and abbreviations that were so foreign to me. I completed my reports, and submitted them to Major Bruce in the morning. Little did I know that the Officer-of-the-Day contacted Major Bruce, and informed him of my actions, and how impressed he was that I looked for a solution to the problem. That was the beginning of a ride for me that would become somewhat magical for the remainder of my Marine Corps career.

First Sergeant Figueroa would soon receive orders back to Vietnam, and he was replaced by the senior man at the school who was Gunnery Sergeant Glen Stiles. "Gunny" Stiles would become a mentor to me that would change my life forever. It was not long before Gunny Stiles received a promotion to Master Sergeant, and he became "Top" to all of us from then on. Top took me under his wing, and started to groom me.

Top Stiles owned a home in town, and his yard had space large enough for a trailer. He decided to buy a trailer, and rent it out, and asked my wife and I to be his tenants, and live there. A brand new trailer to replace the cock-roach infested trailer we were living in? That was a no-brainer, and we took him up on his offer immediately. I not only worked directly with him at the office, but also spent a lot of time with him at home. I was sucking up information from him a mile-a-minute. I was receiving a turbo-charged Marine Corps education about leadership, the Marine Corps, and success.

Each week, the Recruit Training Regiment sent several recruits to the school, who were on their Mess and Maintenance week. They would perform various tasks needed at the school. I was the person in charge of the recruits, and one day I was feeling my oats a little, and tried my best to emulate a drill instructor. The recruits had made some errors on previous tasks, and I decided to chew them out, "DI style". I took them outside of the building, and began to chew them out. After each negative barrage I gave them I would follow it with "Okay?" When I was done I sent them back to their areas, and returned to the building. Top Stiles came to me, and said he had watched me chewing the privates out, and had a suggestion for me: "Never, ever, give a command, and then follow it with 'Okay': if they say 'No', then where can you go with it? Instead, always end it with: *'Do you understand?'*" This was one of many valuable lessons I would learn from Top.

I had quickly been promoted to Lance Corporal within a few months of arrival. I was rapidly gaining the respect of the instructors at the school due to my work on their reports. I often was given rough drafts handed to me by the instructors, and was able to take the roughs, and articulate accurate reviews of the students who were under review. If I got behind I would have my wife Melody come to the office with me at night, and we would work on getting all the typing done. I did whatever it took to make the job work.

In those days, there were no copiers like we have today. If there was a copy needed, we had to put carbon paper over a second or third piece of paper, and then type the material. I was very fortunate that the typewriter I had at my disposal was a state-of-the-art IBM Selectric that had a rotating ball that whirled around at lightning speed. There were no keys as were found in a conventional typewriter. Typing was one of the key tasks in this job. I was very good at typing, being both very fast, and very accurate. I was beginning to appreciate a decision I made in my senior year in high school that was made mostly as a lark: a few of my friends had to choose an elective course. We pondered the usual "guy-class" options such as auto shop, metal shop, wood-working shop, etc. Then it occurred to me: "There are no *girls* in those classes! Where were the girls in a class that we guys could endure? They were in *typing* class." So with that in mind, we selected typing as our elective. It turned out that typing was a natural thing for me, probably because of my skill at guitar playing, and the finger dexterity required to play which was very similar to typing skills. In any event, that decision I attribute to being one of the best decisions I ever made, based on how it made a difference at this very point of my life, and the subsequent changes that would occur in the future.

Within six months of arrival, I was nominated for a meritorious promotion to corporal. I had to go in front of a board, and answer the questions they had for the nominees. The finalists had been boiled down to a choice of between another lance corporal, and me. When it was my turn I smartly marched in, stopped squarely in front of the captain's desk, and snapped to the position of attention. I was then asked a series of questions by both the captain, and the company first sergeant. Everything seemed to go well, until they dismissed me. Procedure calls for taking one step to the rear, doing an about-face, and then marching out of the office smartly. I made a mental error—I stepped back *three* paces, and awkwardly at that, then did my about-face, and marched out. I knew then and there that I blew it. Later I was informed that the other guy got the promotion. A few hours later I ran into him, and he was very smug to me, and I really resented his smugness. As a corporal now, he was senior to me since I was only a lance corporal. However, the seniority of a rank is based on the date of promotion. In the case of a meritorious promotion, the date of the promotion is the day of the actual promotion, whereas regular promotions were always dated at the first day of the month for which the promotion was granted. About one week later I was informed that I was selected for promotion to corporal on the regular promotional basis. Although it did not have the pizzazz of being meritoriously promoted, I ended up being "senior" to my smug competitor who, by virtue of his meritorious promotion date, he ended up being about two weeks *junior* to me.

By the time I had been in the Marine Corps sixteen months I decided that maybe I should volunteer to go to Vietnam. I figured that, as a clerk, I probably would not be on the front lines, and would not be there long due to the short term left on my enlistment. By this time in my career I was being motivated heavily by the great NCO leaders that I was surrounded by. So I walked into the headquarters office and approached the Company First Sergeant, and told him I wanted to volunteer for service in Vietnam. He looked at me and started laughing! "There is no way I am going to let go of you, Corporal Stoner—you are way too valuable to us at the DI School." Despite the rejection of my request, at that moment I also felt like I had arrived.

Parris Island, and the nearby town of Beaufort, are located in swampy environments that are extremely hot, and humid in the summer, and bitter cold in the winter. The bugs there are *incredible*. There are cockroaches two to three inches long, and they have *wings!* They are so large they could carry away a small baby. On top of that, there are huge daddy long-leg spiders that hang down from the trees that are everywhere. They hang about face-high from their webs. There was nothing like getting out of your car in the dark, walking toward the house, and then *squish*—a spider kicks you in your face. Even tough guy Marines had a limit. My wife hated the bugs there, and could never get used to the heat and humidity. It was so humid that you could get out of a shower, towel off, and never get completely dry.

The more I learned about the Marine Corps, the more I liked about what it took to be a drill instructor, and being a leader. Top Stiles continued to work on me. By now, we had another Director at the school by the name of Major Austin. He was mellower than Major Bruce had been, and he also liked me, and what I was doing to make the system work smoothly at the school. Between Major Austin, and Top Stiles, I had two of the finest leaders surrounding me, and constantly inputting me with information. I was getting a base of knowledge that some Marines don't acquire in a career with the Marines.

My original goal when I joined the Marines was to evade the draft, get an administrative job, and not go to Vietnam. It was pretty simple, but almost impossible to achieve during these times. However, to that point in time, I had achieved my goal one hundred percent. I still had eight months left on my enlistment, and my time was getting shorter for getting my discharge, and going home. But, as things would be, this was not going to be the result.

I continued to think about the Marine Corps, and all the things that I had learned so far, I wanted to play a bigger part in the process. I had seen so many students come and go at the school. Many went on to be drill instructors. I remembered my own DI's, and the impact they had on me. I saw the instructors at the school, and the leadership and bearing they had, and how sharp they always looked. I had listened to their stories about what it takes to be a successful Marine drill instructor. The wheels in my head began to turn.

I began to research information at the school about re-enlistment options. I found that if I re-enlisted I could pick up going to Drill Instructor School as an option. There were other perks too: I could select a duty station option as well. I talked it over with my wife Melody. I had to make a commitment to enlist three more years to get these options. It was a huge risk to take based on my goal of not wanting to be involved in the Vietnam War. If I did not make it through the Drill Instructor School I would most certainly be sent to Vietnam, and unlike when I asked to go with only eight months left on my enlistment, I would now have *three years left*. There were other risks as well: I could not attend the Parris Island Drill Instructor School because it would be a conflict of interest for the instructors. The bias was untenable. I would have to attend the Drill Instructor School at San Diego, which was my duty station choice anyway. But the risk was based on the competition between the two schools: I would be attending *their* school as an insider from the *other* school. There was the potential for the San Diego school to try and embarrass the Parris Island school if I did not make it. They could easily push me to limits beyond normal. This was a very real risk for me. I discussed the options with Top Stiles and Major Austin. However, the lure of being a drill instructor, and being considered one of the top two percent of Marine Corps NCOs, was too much to lose. I re-enlisted 8 months before my first enlistment was up, and was scheduled to attend the very next Drill Instructor School class starting in December, 1969, at Marine Corps Recruit Depot, San Diego.

Before I left Parris Island I received a Meritorious Mast from the Commanding General of MCRD. My services at the Drill Instructor School were outlined as outstanding, and I had exceeded the realm of my duties by learning and mastering the functions of that job, and did a job that was without parallel. It was a fitting send-off to my new duties.

Melody and I left the heat and humidity of Parris Island and headed across the country toward arid San Diego to begin a new chapter in our lives.

PART TWO:

THE DRILL FIELD

DRILL INSTRUCTOR SCHOOL: BOOT CAMP AGAIN

The Marine Corps drill instructor is one of the premier icons of the Marine Corps. Every single recruit that passes through the depot gates at Parris Island, South Carolina, and San Diego, California, has had a drill instructor. The drill instructor makes such an impression on the recruit that they never forget their drill instructors names, voices, or faces. His look, his voice, his bearing—all indelibly etched deeply into the memory banks of all that were under his leadership.

No single person or entity in the Marines will have more influence on recruits or young Marines than a drill instructor. For this reason, the Marine Corps only wanted the very best men for this job. The screening process is intense—many aspects of a Marine NCO were probed. Military bearing, leadership qualities, and command presence, were all areas that the reviewing committee were looking at when deciding whether to accept or reject a candidate. A committee interview was conducted as the final means of determining if a candidate was going to be accepted or rejected.

Many of the candidates in the late 1960's and early 1970's were NCOs that were returning from Vietnam duty. A tour in Vietnam was typically thirteen months, during that period. A lot can happen to a Marine in thirteen months in a crazy war zone like Vietnam. Most of those Marines saw combat action. Many saw their friends killed, or maimed, in action. Most of these men were affected by this war in some way, or another. They were all tired men, who were happy to be alive, and back in a safe environment. Some really looked forward to the experience of being a drill instructor so that they could instill their experiences to the recruits to make them better Marines. Others did not feel as lucky to be assigned to the school, as the drill field was often perceived as one of the toughest and most grueling jobs in the Marine Corps—these men wanted to kick back for a while after returning from Vietnam. No matter what their personal desire was, once accepted to the school they were in, and they had to deal with it.

I was the most junior man in my class. By the time my class started I had been in the Marine Corps a grand total of only nineteen months. I was still just a corporal when I checked in to the school. I received a promotion to sergeant shortly after arriving. I had only one ribbon on my blouse—most of the Marines in my class had row upon row of ribbons awarded for various acts of bravery, or campaigns they had participated in. From a personal standpoint, I felt like I was out-gunned in every area. The magnitude of the battle I faced was sinking in rapidly as I saw the other men I would be competing with at the school. Not only was I the most inexperienced, and junior of the class, I came directly from the Drill Instructor School at Parris Island—a competitor to this school. I felt certain coolness toward me, and there were some who thought I may have somehow pulled a few strings to get in. I knew they were going to make it tough on me. But failure was not an option for me—I had too much at stake here, and failure just could not be accepted. I could not let my Marine friends at DI School, Parris Island down. They put their trust in me that I could do this, and I was going to get through this, no matter what. Not to mention that I had re-enlisted for 3 more years to get into this school, and if I failed, then I would most certainly be sent to Vietnam, negating my original goal in the first place to not serve in Vietnam due to my personal opposition to that war. I had lots at stake here.

I was probably a little more prepared for the events of the school than most of the other students due to my previous role as the Chief Clerk at the Parris Island school. I knew of the psychological element, and what the instructors were up to, and what they were trying to evoke from the students. But, knowing what was coming ahead, and then dealing with it, was two totally different things.

My class had about sixty students when we started. I knew that the total would be much less by graduation day. Attrition was a normal part of the process. Some of the candidates would be determined to not have the necessary skills, or qualities needed to continue. Time would tell.

DI School was very much like boot camp was for recruits. Basically the same things were covered. The major difference was that the students at the school were all NCOs and Staff NCOs, and were going to be treated as such. Most of us were married, and went home at night. All of us had to maintain a bunk at the school. We had to maintain our living quarters, and they were inspected every day. Everything had to be perfect! The bunk sheets had to have forty-five degree angles where the ends fold down, and there had to be an exact four inches of sheet showing where it folded back over the blanket. The blanket had to be so tight that a dime would bounce up if it were dropped in the middle of the bed. There could be no Irish penants (loose ends or material) down under the mattress. Our wall locker had to have our uniforms hanging perfectly. The footlocker had to be arranged correctly.

The school taught courses on every subject that the recruits would be getting: history, first aid, M-14 rifle, .45 caliber pistol, hygiene, etc. We would soon be teaching recruits, so it was imperative that we knew the subjects cold. We were going to be tested on these, and had to pass the exams in order to pass the course.

One of the areas that were most concentrated on at DI School was close order drill. All of us students at the school were familiar with drill—after all, we all went through boot camp, and had to drill as recruits. Most of the students had many years of experience in the Marine Corps and had either been subject to close order drill, or had conducted it. But knowing how to drill, and teaching close order drill, was two very different beasts. Every movement in close order drill can be broken down to individual movements. We had to memorize these individual movements. We also had to demonstrate our ability to articulate those movements in verbal communications. Hours would be spent practicing each position and verbalizing them. It had to be right. This one section alone may have been the most responsible for the attrition of the students from the school. Some students just could not get this down.

I saw first-hand at the school what the affects of war had on men. During a class on the .45 caliber automatic pistol, the instructor was going over the nomenclature, and features of the pistol. Students were taking notes, and paying attention. He was discussing the trigger pull to the class, and asked a student to step up, and estimate how many pounds of pressure he thought the trigger-pull actually was. Eager to show his knowledge, the sergeant jumped up, took the pistol in his hand, and pulled back on the trigger. *Bang!* The pistol discharged. With the exception of me, every single person seated in the room dove for cover at the sound of the pistol going off, as though they were still in Vietnam, and incoming rounds were landing! It was a surreal sight. Once everyone regained their composure, the instructor reamed out the sergeant who pulled the trigger for not first checking to see if the pistol was loaded, which was rule # 1 when handling *any* weapon. Of course the instructor knew in advance what would happen, and the result was a great lesson for us all. But for me, the lesson was even more valuable, as I was seeing first-hand how wars affected people.

The school stressed physical fitness training (PT). PT was very important, as we were going to be out in front of our recruits doing PT, and we had to be in shape in order to lead. Every day we spent at least one hour doing PT, followed by a three mile run. The school director was a very fast runner, and he would lead the platoon. PT was probably the second most common reason men dropped out of training—some men just could not keep up the pace.

Inspections were abundant at the school. Sometimes we had a surprise inspection of our squad bay areas while we were in class. I always felt fairly safe with those inspections because I was living at home at nights, and did not use my bunk, so it was always in good shape, and ready for an inspection. Or so I thought! One day, we returned from one of the classes upstairs, and found the squad bay totally upside down. Bunks pulled over, foot lockers askew, and our stuff was everywhere. Blankets were ripped off the bunks. It looked like a cyclone hit us. We had obviously failed our surprise inspection. From that point forward, I spent a little more time each morning making sure that my area was perfect.

Every morning we also had a uniform inspection. Our uniforms had to be absolutely perfect. Our blouses and trousers had to be ironed to perfection. We would get the uniforms back from the cleaners, and then start from scratch, re-pressing the uniform with our irons. The instructors showed us how to make new creases so that they were razor sharp, and perfectly straight. The cleaners never got them correct to the standards required of the school. The utility uniforms came back from the cleaners with starch so heavy they could stand up by themselves. But, they too had to be re-ironed. We made special solutions of starch that we sprayed on the utility uniforms, and then ironed in new creases, and pleats. We were totally anal about our uniforms, as the inspectors were not going to let a single item slip by them. The starched utilities actually had sheen to them when we were done. There could not be a single thread sticking out. We went over the uniforms with a magnifying glass to make sure they were right. Hours would be spent spit-shining our boots and shoes, resulting in a gloss that can best be described as something that you could shave by using the reflective surface like a mirror. We looked sharp at those inspections. But, somehow they always seemed to find something.

Another of the areas that the school spent considerable time on was the subject of the "SOP" which stood for Standard Operating Procedure. The SOP was the bible of how to do things. It was the rules by which we had to strictly adhere to. The Marine Corps had an SOP for everything it does. There was a rule for everything. In recruit training, the SOP was the guidelines we had to live by every single day. Any violation of the SOP was grounds for immediate dismissal from the drill field, and the violator would likely end up being court-martialed over the infraction. The single, most important matter covered, was that we absolutely could not *maltreat* the recruits. There were limits as to how much PT could be issued, depending on phase of training. Anything we needed to know about recruit training could be found in the SOP. We were constantly drilled on the rules we would have to live by, and they made it abundantly clear to all of us, that under no circumstances would violating these rules ever be tolerated. Not ever. The more I learned about the rules, the more I realized how my very own DI's had violated them. Sort of an irony I guess—too bad I didn't know then what I knew now.

Attending the school took about eighteen to twenty hours of work per day to succeed. There was little time for sleep, or family, during this time. That was something I would soon learn was also what we would be facing on the drill field.

When it was all said and done, this was second as the most grueling thing I ever went through, with boot camp itself as the leader. We were put to the test on everything we did for the entire time we were there. The instructors wanted to ensure that those that graduated from the course were only the most qualified men, who could handle the grueling day-to-day activities, and stresses of being a drill instructor.

About sixty percent of the men that started the school were there at the end. Before graduating, we spent a couple of nights in the field with actual drill instructors. It was there that we were told that we would learn how to do things the "right way" when we got to the field. I sensed that there was more learning to do. I also realized that there seemed to be two ways of doing things—the right way by the SOP, and *"the way they did things on the field."*

Upon graduating, we were then assigned to a specific battalion, and company. One at a time we were told where we were to report to. They did it alphabetical, as usual, so I had to wait until almost the end before I was to learn of my destiny. I could have died when I heard my assignment—Charlie Company, First Battalion! That was the same company and battalion I had just graduated from boot camp only twenty-one months earlier. I was blown away even more when I checked in to Charlie Company. I was being assigned to platoon 1037, and they were located in the *same* Quonset huts that I had been a recruit in. But even crazier—I was replacing my very own drill instructor, Sergeant Christian who had been relieved for violations of the SOP.

I gazed around at the area and I had a strange feeling. There I was, standing with a campaign cover on my head, looking at the same huts I had slept in; the same place that I had been told of the assassination of Robert Kennedy during the California Presidential Primary; the place where I first felt like crying on my first night. So many memories of being a recruit filled my mind.

I had now come full circle in my Marine Corps world: I was now right back to the same place that I had started from.

PUT THE JAM ON—FAST

During the late 1960's and early 1970's, taking a brand new platoon to their first meal at the mess hall was an experience most Marine recruits will never forget. Many of the recruits had traveled long distances to get to MCRD. Most of them arrived early in the evening, and were processed through Receiving Barracks where they were issued their initial military issue of necessary items. They then were released to their new drill instructors around 0230 (2:30 AM) in the morning. By the time they had been herded over to their new living quarters, and made up their racks (bunks) it was around 0330 (3:30 AM). They were put to bed, and then after only an hour of sleep at best, they were woken up at 0430 (4:30 AM) to get them to the mess hall. New recruits were the first to go through the mess hall in the daily chow schedule.

Everything in the Marine Corps boot camp system was going to be a learning experience for recruits. I have always been a believer in the learning philosophy that says "When a pupil was ready, the teacher appeared, and not one second sooner." What that meant was that people must be *ready* to learn, and if they are not ready, they will not learn. That sometimes meant that the learning experience was going to be a slow and hard experience for some.

Since the Marines are a fighting unit it was going to be necessary to teach recruits to do things that they may be required to do in combat. Eating rapidly was important in combat. One of the things they must learn for combat was following orders. And that meant following orders *instantly*, without delay, and without thinking about the orders. That may seem like a simple task, but most recruits had not grown up to respond to orders quickly.

The average age of a recruit during the Vietnam era was approximately seventeen years old. He had an average education level of the tenth grade. Many were directed to join the Marine Corps by a judge, or go to jail. These were times when youth of that era were doing more protesting and rebelling than anything else. The typical recruit, when probed, would admit that he joined the Marines to become a man—all based on the advertising motto "The Marine Corps builds men." Based on that, it was common sense that the recruits did not yet perceive themselves to being men, and needed something to establish that.

Young people were generally under the direct management of their parents, and were willing to obey the rules that were imposed—right up to the point in their lives that their hormones kicked in, and they began to convert from children to youth. At that stage in young men's lives they started to develop independence, and began to rebel against the authority that they had once been willing to obey while they were younger. Rebelling was absolutely a normal part of being a youth. But during these times it was a little different than any other era in our history: this was the *Vietnam era*. People were opposed to the war. Americans were rebelling against the war. Colleges held campus-wide protests. Every day, in just about every newspaper, one could read a story about a significant protest taking place. Protesting the war. Protesting big government, and just protesting for the sake of protesting. Young people no longer trusted their parents, the government, or any other form of authority.

The youth of that era were raised without a lot of responsibility. Their mothers made their beds, washed their clothes, cooked their meals, and probably even did their homework for them. They were not often given responsibilities that would begin to teach them how to be responsible adults later on. Things were handed to them. Whatever these kids wanted their parents obliged. These youth were spoiled, and were used to getting their way.

So there they were in my Marine Corps. They knew that the going was to be tough, but they were going to find out, a little at a time, how really tough it was going to be.

At the mess hall we would instruct them how to go through the line and what the rules were: "First, you take the fork, knife, spoon, and a tray. Then you follow through the line and put the tray out for whatever food items you want. Whatever you take, you are required to eat—this is not home. We do not waste food in the Marine Corps. When you have received your food, you will take your trays to a table, and when the table is full, you will sit down, eat your food, and not talk. No food can be taken from the mess hall. Most important: *when the last person through the line is done, you must all leave, taking your trays to the cleaning drop area.*" That last rule was very important.

The recruits were starving at that point. To them, eating did not require rules, and they were *not listening*. They were not yet ready for learning our ways. So, they went through the lines picking up forks, knives, spoons and trays. They placed their trays out for the food offered, and they filled their trays with food.

They went to their tables, waited for the table to reach capacity, and then they all sat down at once, and began to eat.

I was the last one to go through the chow line. I took my food to my table. I sat down, and I ate my food. But I was a fast eater—*very fast!* In a flash, I was done. I looked at the platoon—many were still applying the jam to their toast—they looked like they were dining at Denny's. I stood up, and hollered: "*I am done. Now get out. Now!*" They looked around incredulously. They had barely begun to eat. I gave them a reminder: "*I said get up, and get out. You are done. There better not be any uneaten food on those trays when you put those trays down for cleaning!*"

They still could not believe it. They were rising, and moving rapidly toward the tray drop area, eating their food on the fly. I moved down to the tray drop, and I made it well known that they could not leave any food on the trays. I yelled for them to hurry up and to get moving. They were now becoming more ready to "learn". The next time we eat, they would eat to a different cadence.

There was another rule that some of the recruits did not listen to. In a hurry to clear their trays, and fearing they would starve to death, they put some food in their pockets for a snack later. As soon as the recruits left the mess hall they fell into platoon formation outside. At that point we would walk down each row to spot those recruits that had extra items in their pockets. Food outside of the mess hall was considered contraband. Those recruits that had taken food out of the mess hall were given a heavy dose of incentive PT (hard physical training exercises, often used for disciplinary purposes) when we returned to the area. The recruits were slowly getting the idea of how things were going to be.

FIRST TIME FOR
A LOT OF THINGS

After arriving at the receiving barracks, the recruits were issued everything they would need to survive boot camp. Some of the issued items were things that the recruits were not accustomed to using: a safety razor was one of those items.

During the Vietnam era, safety razors did not come with multiple blades as they do today: they came with one blade. I guess the reason they were called "safety razors" was because the blade was contained inside the shaver housing in such a manner that the blade could only cut a certain depth before it would hit the razor housing, thus limiting the potential for a deep, life-threatening slice that could be made with a straight-edge razor. Most recruits had been raised using electric shavers, if they even shaved at all. What a shock it was for them to find out that they were going to be using safety razors instead. Their shaving kit also came with a can of foam shaving cream.

The first showers the recruits had after being assigned to their platoons would occur on the second night at MCRD. The showers were in wooden buildings, a short distance from the Quonset huts, and were located next to the heads. The inside of the shower room was roughly devoted to two thirds of the area having wash basins with a mirror over them, and the other one third of the room was the shower area consisting of about nine or ten spigots. The water was often not real hot, and the drains were usually partially plugged up, resulting in water standing up to six inches deep on the deck of the shower area. Each platoon was assigned a time to use the shower room, so it was necessary for the platoon to get in and out very quickly. The process began with us shouting an order: *"On the road in shower uniform in one minute!"* The recruits would then strip down to their skivvies, and a pair of thong sandals that were called "shower shoes". They would bring one of the towels they were issued, as well as their shaving kit. The kit also had a bar of soap, a tooth brush, and toothpaste. The platoon would be marched up to the shower building. One squad at a time would be ordered into the shower room and given a time limit to shower and shave: normally around five minutes. We told them to not speak, and to get out before the time limit was up.

For some reason, the recruits always felt that they were secure in the shower area, and they would often start talking, or grabassing around. But, we were ready! Without hesitation we would jump in the water with our spit-shined shoes and straight creases in our uniforms, and start yelling: *"You ladies were told not to not talk. What the hell are you talking for? Turn the hot water off, and stand there in the cold water. All of you report to the Duty Office when you get done with your showers!"* The recruits were stunned to see that their drill instructors jumped into the water, ruining their uniforms and shoes. They were going to be even more chagrined when they got to the Duty Office, and found out they were going to be doing some extensive incentive training in what they would soon learn to hate: a place called the "Pit" which was the dirt area outside the Duty Hut where the recruits would be given endless incentive training in the form of physical training (PT).

Shaving under the time-gun with a new shaving device was not a good idea if you wanted to avoid cuts. But avoiding that scenario was not in the cards for the recruits, and they were forced to shave quickly, and under *enormous* pressure. One by one they would leave the shower rooms with faces bleeding from multiple cuts from their new razors. We would tell them to take some tissue, and apply a small piece over the wounds to coagulate the blood. Worse, some of them did not do a good job of cutting the facial hair off and they still had stubble on their faces, resulting in their being told to go back, and shave again. Those recruits were going to have to learn how to get clean-shaven with those shavers. It would require many cuts and nicks on their faces, but eventually the recruits would learn the technique of proper shaving.

At home, the recruit was often taken care of by his mother. She probably did everything for him: washed clothes, make his bed, etc. But, in boot camp there was no mom to do that. About one week after the recruits first came to the platoon, they would be marched to the wash racks to learn how to wash their clothes. The recruits would have to take their bucket, put some of the detergent they were issued into it, and fill it with water from the wash racks. They would first put their whites skivvies into the bucket to soak them, and then each piece would be placed on the cement wash rack, and scrubbed with the scrub brush the recruits were also issued. They would learn to thoroughly rinse out each piece, and then ring it out to remove as much of the water as possible. Next, they would take their green utility clothes, and green socks, and put them in the bucket to soak. Each piece would also be scrubbed, rinsed, and rung out. The greens would bleed their colors out at first. The recruits would then have to carry their wet clothes in their buckets to the clothes lines, and hang them, using the clothes pins they were issued to keep them on the lines. One recruit was always kept at the clothes line area to keep guard on the platoon clothing while they dried. For almost all the recruits, that was something they had never done before. When the clothes were dry they would retrieve them, and take them back to their Quonset huts, and fold them neatly before putting them away in their footlockers. Recruits were starting to understand that Marines were clean and neat, and that nothing would ever compromise that.

Once a week the recruits were issued one clean sheet, and a clean pillow case. The recruits would take the bottom sheet on their racks, and turn them in for cleaning. They would take last week's top sheet, and put it on the bottom, and use the new sheet as the top sheet. That was a practical means of keeping costs down. The bottom sheet is the one that got the dirtiest, so that was the one that was replaced.

Every platoon always had a bed-wetter. It was hard to believe that a young man in his late teens would still be wetting the bed at night, but the fact was, there was one in every platoon. Those recruits were very problematic as bed-wetting was not going to be acceptable, and they *had* to be cured. Every time the recruit wet the bed his mattress and linens had to be aired out on a special mattress rack outside. There were several procedures that we normally used to cure the bed wetter. The first thing we did was to have the bed wetter take an upper bunk, and then we put the largest and meanest recruit from his squad in the bunk below him. Sometimes that was all that it would take. The next step, if needed, was to have the recruit woken every half-hour at night by the fire-watch, and then marched to the head to urinate—each time it had to be logged by the fire-watch. It also helped that the recruit would receive a certain amount of public humiliation. Every occurrence reported would cause the Drill instructor to call out: *"Private Bed-Wetter to the Duty Office, now!"* Each squad would repeat that order, and then the private had to come to the Duty Office to be rendered his incentive PT in the Pit. With the recruit under pressure from the recruit beneath him, the constant marching to the head every half-hour at night, and the public humiliation we put him through; he would normally be cured of his problem. I never witnessed a failure with those techniques.

TWO LEFT BOOTS

The first week of recruit life at MCRD was for processing. During that week many important initial activities took place. Aptitude testing was given to determine the fields the recruits would eventually be assigned to. Medical exams were made to double check physical eligibility and to start the inoculation process for the vaccinations recruits would need. Dental exams revealed those recruits that would need dental work. Clothing and equipment needed for training were issued.

One of the most important elements of the first week was the indoctrination of Marine Corps ways. We drill instructors had perhaps our biggest impact on the new recruit during processing week. The recruit joined the Marine Corps to become a man, and had preconceived ideas about how things were going to go. But nothing in his imagination could have prepared him for the initial shock of the methods used by neither the drill instructors nor their intensity every minute of the day.

The recruit quickly discovered that practically nothing he or his platoon peers did would be good enough or fast enough for his ever-present DI's. We caught what seemed to be every single little error that was made. At no point in the recruit's life prior to boot camp had anyone been in his face with such intensity as we were. Our strategy was to keep the recruits off-guard at all times. We would create constant chaos using enormous amounts of yelling and screaming. The atmosphere we created put every recruit into a state of stress that removed their individuality of thought. They suddenly were responding to orders. They had no will to question those orders and especially the person who gave them!

We had established complete control. There were no exceptions. We would expect an immediate response to our orders. We meant *now* when we gave an order. Any recruit that did not respond instantly found a drill instructor inches from his face yelling at him to hurry up. We often were so close to the recruits' face when yelling at him that our Smokey-the-Bear hat brim was all that kept our faces from touching the face of the recruit. The voice of a drill instructor would send chills down the back of even the largest and most macho recruit. To the recruits, we looked ten feet tall with our campaign cover on. We were bigger than big, larger than large. We were a grisly bear and the recruits were our dinner.

Recruits had instantly learned to try at all costs to remain as invisible as they could—avoid any contact with us. It had now become crystal clear that perfection was the only acceptable result. We were not going to compromise on *anything*. They had realized that, within moments of arrival, they were going to be doing things differently than ever before: that would be *our way*, the *drill instructors' way*.

The recruits were also introduced to physical training (PT). Physical training was used for more than just building up the body. As drill instructors we were authorized to use PT as "incentive training" to make recruits pay for any action deemed needed to instill discipline. The public image of "drop and give me ten" was mild to say the least compared to the punishments doled out by us. Fortunately for the recruits, the Marine Corps SOP (Standard Operating Procedure) placed a limit as to how much PT we could issue to a recruit during each of the phases of training. Many of us turned a blind eye to the limitations. The most often-used exercise used for incentive training PT was the "bend and thrust". That exercise started from the recruit standing in an upright position. The first step was to bend down and place their hands on the deck. The second step was to kick the feet straight back keeping the legs straight in the process. Step three was to kick the legs back to the original position as in step one. Step four would require rising straight up. The recruit was to sound off each step: "One, sir; two, sir; three, sir; one, sir! Step number four was never called out as number "four", rather using that step number as the unit count. So if the recruit was told to do twenty-five bends and thrusts step four would keep track of the count. The recruit would call out these counts either individually if they alone were issued the PT, or in-unison if the platoon or a small group were called out. Everyone was in unison—or everyone started over.

With all the yelling, PT, and other stresses the recruits were encountering they were also going through changes in metabolism. It was not uncommon for recruits not to be able to take a bowel movement for up to a week after arrival. Some of that was also caused by the fact that there was no privacy in boot camp. The commodes were in an open room—no walls, no doors. Most recruits had never had to deal with lack of privacy. Suddenly, all of those around them were privy to their most private functions. Of course we didn't help that issue—head calls were not something that went without some extra pressure. The acts of going to the bathroom in the Marine Corps were called "head calls", and were usually authorized in terms of "time allowed". For example, we would command: "Head calls in order for thirty seconds!" That meant that a squad had thirty seconds to complete their head call, not thirty-one seconds! The other squads were doing a count-down from thirty: "Thirty, twenty-nine, twenty-eight ..." Every recruit had to be out of the head by the end of the count-down or they were going to be facing an angry DI and we would make them do a *lot of PT*. It did not take a recruit long to learn how to complete his personal business in a very short amount of time.

The recruit state-of-mind was being scrambled to the point where they were not always thinking straight.

Initial clothing issue was when the recruits got their first issue of the clothing needed to complete the first phases of training. It consisted of being issued a total of two more pairs of trousers (the first pair was issued on the first night), three utility shirts that the Marines call "blouses", a utility cap (called a cover), and two pairs of boots. Clothing issue was not like going to Macy's and trying on items in a dressing room. Rather, it was going down a line where clothing issuers stood on the other side of a counter and literally threw the clothing items at a recruit who yelled out his waist size, neck size, shoe size, etc. The recruits had been given a quick measurement of their waists and neck sizes prior to going through this clothing gauntlet so they knew what to yell out. All items issued would be tried on later at the platoon areas.

The clothing issued often had to be altered by the recruits to fit properly. Most trouser legs were way too long and would require the recruit to hem them up. Recruits were issued a basic sewing kit known as a "John Wayne". That kit contained threads in both khaki color and drab olive green color. It also contained several needles. Recruits were rapidly discovering that being in the Marines was not just going to be shooting weapons—a little sewing would also be in order.

As soon as the clothing was issued the platoon returned to their Quonset hut area. It would be important for us to inspect the recruits' issues to make sure they got the correct amount of each garment and that the clothing fit reasonably well. It was not uncommon for a recruit, being in the scrambled frame of mind that they were in, to return and not have been given everything they needed. We would have a footlocker placed outside the Duty Hut and would have the recruits step up on the footlocker, one at a time, and we made sure the items fit. Usually, we would have them start with the utility blouses first. Three times the recruits went through the line. If everyone had the correct issue of three then they went to the next item of issue. Trousers were next. That would take more time because the

DI's were going to have to tell each recruit how much they would have to hem the trouser legs. Again, two times through the line with the new issue and then one more time for the trousers issued at the receiving barracks.

The most important items checked were the boots. It was absolutely necessary that the boots fit properly from the start or the recruit was going to have foot issues that could affect his ability to function properly. So the boots were the last and most-checked clothing items. The recruits were told to go inside their Quonset huts and put on their first pair of boots, lace them up and return for the inspection. One by one they came and stepped up on the footlocker while we checked each and every boot. If there were any issues with the fit the recruits were sent back to the clothing issue center for better fitting new boots. Things normally went smoothly during the inspections, but there could be twists. One recruit I was inspecting appeared on my footlocker wearing two *right* boots. I couldn't believe it! I yelled at the private: *"You idiot! What in the hell are you doing wearing two right boots?"* He replied "Sir, there must have been a mix up and the private was issued two right boots, Sir!" I immediately got right into his face and screamed: *"Private—get your dumb ass back inside and get the other boots and get back here right away. Do you understand me?"* "Sir, yes sir!" and off he went to the Quonset hut. Moments later he was back. He jumped up on the footlocker, this time wearing two *left* boots. In a very exasperated voice he said: "Sir, the private's other two boots were *two left boots*, sir!"

Stress could clearly affect clear thinking.

HOUSE MICE AND
THE KING RAT

Drill instructor duty had a few perks. The busy duties we had kept us going just about every minute of our day. Keeping the duty hut in a neat and orderly fashion became the duty of the recruits as part of their normal house-cleaning activities.

Those duties fell to the positions known as "House Mice". The House Mice came in and swept the floors, made our racks up. They put on clean sheets, etc. They were overseen by the "King Rat". King Rat positions required a responsible recruit who was also not absolutely intimidated by the presence of the four drill instructors that occupied the Duty Hut. They also had to be trustworthy because they sometimes would be in a position to overhear things from us that were not to be relayed to the other recruits.

The process of finding a proper group for that role was sometimes difficult to get the right ones. In one of my early platoons I had a private by the name of Private Epstein. He was a very smart young man with more education than the average recruit. I liked his style. He had an interesting sound too: a New York Yiddish twang. We were in our first week of training, and that was when we named our House Mice, and the King Rat, to our staff. Private Epstein impressed me over the other two at that point, and he was almost a sure lock for the job. We were about one or two days away from naming the King Rat, but we needed a little more observation first.

Boot camp protocol called for recruits who wished to speak to their drill instructor who was inside the Duty Hut, to first stand at attention at the base of the open hatch (door), and then pound on the hatch three times very loudly, and say: "Sir, Private So and So, Platoon 1015, requests permission to enter the Duty Hut, Sir!" At that point a typical response from us would be *"I hear a woodpecker!"* The recruit would then have to repeat the process, only the second time pounding on the spot on the door much more loudly. In reality, it was common for that process to be repeated numerous times. When the private was finally pounding brutally on the hatch, we might respond to his verbal request with: *"I can't hear you!"*, and then the process started all over. When we were finally satisfied with the quality of the pounding on the hatch, and the verbal request being loud enough, we would grant permission to enter the Duty Hut. The private would then smartly march forward, and do a facing movement to squarely place him centered in front of our desk. The recruit would then have to request permission to speak: "Sir, Pvt So and So, Platoon 1015, requests permission to speak to the drill instructor, Sir!" We would almost always say *"I can't hear you!"*, and the process would be repeated again until we were satisfied with the volume. At that point the recruit would be granted permission to speak to us. The whole time he was talking to us he had to remain at the position of attention, with his head and eyes straight ahead, and not ever looking down at us sitting below his eye level. It was a natural human action for the eyes to look toward the person being spoken to, so in First Phase that was another common recruit error: "eyeballing the drill instructor." That most certainly would get us up and out of our chair, and into the face of the recruit in the blink-of-an-eye. The whole purpose of that drill was to make the recruit think, act boldly, and in a disciplined manner. Repetition was needed to accomplish that.

The House Mice had just left the duty office one morning, having completed their morning chores. I was doing some file work on the recruit records that we kept. The recruits were in their Quonset huts policing their areas, and getting ready for another full day of training.

Bang, bang, bang, went the rap on the hatch. "Sir, Pvt Smith, Platoon 1015, requests permission to enter the Duty Office, Sir!" *"I hear a woodpecker"* I replied loudly. *Bang. Bang. Bang.* "Sir, Pvt Smith, Platoon 1015, requests permission to enter the duty office, Sir!" *"I still hear a woodpecker!"* was my response again. *Bang! Bang! Bang! "Sir, Private Smith, Platoon 1015, requests permission to enter the Duty Office, Sir!"* "Enter" I responded. Pvt Smith awkwardly stepped up to my desk, and in a very animated way spit out: *"Sir, Private Smith, Platoon 1015, requests permission to speak to the drill instructor, Sir!"* Sensing an odd urgency in his voice, I gave permission. The words he said have lived with me forever: *"Sir, Pvt Epstein just hung himself on his rack, sir!"*

All four drill instructors in the Duty Hut immediately jumped to our feet, and ran to the Quonset hut that Pvt Epstein was billeted in. Sure enough, he was hanging by his belt, which he had tied to the top rail of his rack. He was as white as a sheet of paper, and *not breathing*. We immediately untied the belt and loosened the loop around his neck, then laid him on the deck. We found no pulse;

no breathing. My heart was *pounding*. I could not believe this was happening. Sergeant Wren, a studied expert on first aid, immediately doubled his fists, and then hit the recruit with a heavy blow between his shoulder blades in an effort to get his heart and breathing going again. Nothing happened. Another blow was administered. Still, nothing happened. Finally, on the third blow there was a reaction. Pvt Epstein's pulse came back. He started to breath again. *We* started to breathe again! By that time the medics had arrived with the ambulance. They started giving Private Epstein oxygen, and then, in a flash, he was in the back of the ambulance, and off to the Depot Medical Center for treatment. I figured that would be the last time we saw Private Epstein—he surely would be dropped from training for his obvious psychological problems.

We sighed in relief that we did not have a recruit casualty. I was having a hard time connecting what happened with the recruit it happened to. To think he was just about to be promoted to King Rat. We could never really tell what was going on in a recruits mind.

I decided that from that point going forward I would be more careful about having recruits repeat commands during that phase of training: that kid could have died if another minute had gone by without aid.

To my surprise, Private Epstein was returned to the platoon by the end of the day. The medical crew found nothing wrong with him, and attributed his action to just stressing out. I couldn't believe it: he almost successfully committed suicide, and they felt he was okay? That was the Navy for you!

First Phase of training was a phase that was somewhat designed to keep the recruits off-guard, and to always have them believe that they needed to continue to improve. One of the tests of that was what was referred to as the "Initial Inspection". That was an inspection usually held by the Company Commander who was accompanied by the Series Gunnery Sergeant. During the inspection the inspectors were looking at the presentation of the recruit uniform, cleanliness of the recruit's rifle, and how the recruit answered the questions asked of him. That inspection was destined to find every possible flaw, and expose every incorrect thing. The recruits had worked hard cleaning their rifles, and preparing their uniforms, but we wanted to show them they needed to put in more effort, and to stride to be better prepared next time. There was a lot of tension prior to that inspection—even more than the standard supply of tension that all of us drill instructors had endless supplies of.

The inspection took place in an area that was large enough to conduct some basic drill movements with a platoon. The platoon formation for an inspection was provided by the command "Open Ranks, March!" The squads then march forward in rows, so that each squad had just over twice the normal space between them in order that the inspectors could come between the ranks, and conduct their inspections.

I moved the platoon into position and commanded "Open Ranks, March." The squads moved appropriately forward. The next command was "Cover" wherein the recruits adjusted their alignment so that they were perfectly behind the private in front of them. Once they had covered, they were to remain at the position of attention until they were given another command. Since there was some time involved in the inspection process, it was normal for us to give another command of "Parade Rest", which allowed the recruits to take a more relaxed position than the position of attention, but still required them to remain motionless and looking straight ahead. Having given the command to the platoon I immediately heard a rifle hit the deck, and then heard the horrible plop-sound that can only be made when a person fell flat on his face to the ground. I quickly determined that it was Private Epstein. He had passed out and fallen directly on his face. We ran to him, rolled him over, and his face was a terrible mess. His nose was broken, his teeth were knocked out, and blood was gushing out of his face. Once again the medics came and took Private Epstein away. This time, Private Epstein never came back.

A new search began for a King Rat.

THE PIT

The Quonset huts that were used for billeting during the Vietnam era were lined up in rows, and were separated by about five feet of dirt on all sides. The front of the huts faced a paved roadway that was about eight feet wide or so. The dirt area was known as "grass". More specifically, it was the "drill instructor's grass" and was a sacred area. One of the cardinal rules in boot camp was to *never walk* on the "grass".

Each morning after the morning meal the recruits had to "police" their areas, meaning they had to clean the huts, and the surrounding grass areas. The grass had to be "watered". Certain recruits were assigned the task of taking care of the grass, and were responsible to bring bucket loads of water in from the wash racks, and sprinkle the water on the grass so as to make it very moist to keep the dust levels down. Once the grass was thoroughly watered, they would then take rakes, and rake the grass areas into very neat rows of rake markings. A narrow pathway was tamped down straight down the center of the grass areas so that the drill instructor had a secure area to walk on when the platoon was assembled in formation on the narrow paved road area. Extreme caution was made by recruits to avoid putting any footprints on the raked area as this was tantamount to "walking on the drill instructors' grass", and was a fate worse than death if caught. The same process was repeated in the evening to bring the area back into perfect order after the day's activities.

One of the best tools we had at our disposal to motivate recruits was "incentive training", which was the acceptable physical training (PT) that could be administered to recruits for a variety of offenses, including lack of motivation. The SOP (Standard Operating Procedure) had limits as to how much could be administered at one time during each phase of training. Most of us felt the limits fell way short of the amounts needed to be effective, so there was some very "interpretive" ways of seeing the SOP guidelines. One interpretation was that the exercises had to be done *correctly*. So, no matter how many counts of the exercise were done by the recruit up to any given point, if the we felt they were not being done correctly we could have the recruit start over.

Incentive training could be administered at any location except outside the mess hall, and on the parade deck. The most common area to have the incentive training done was called the "Pit". The Pit was the grass area outside the Quonset huts, or "the drill instructors grass". The incentive training could be administered to the entire platoon if needed, or to individuals, or small groups.

Incentive training was something that most recruits feared, and wanted to avoid at all costs. It was harsh, and very physically punishing. When the recruits were finally done with the PT, they were physically spent.

We would call the offending recruits to the Duty Hut, and review briefly what they had done wrong. Then we would tell them to get in the Pit. A typical order to recruits would be: "Get in the Pit private and give me thirty repetitions of bends and thrusts. Ready, begin!" At that the recruit began the exercise, and counted each count of the four count exercise with the final count the actual number of repetitions completed: "One sir, two sir, three sir, *one* sir; one sir, two sir, three sir, *two* sir; and this would continue until he reached the full count issued. Usually we would intercept the recruit toward the end of the count, and say "I can't hear you. Start over!" And the process would then begin all over. The more repetitions, the more they would sweat. The sweat would mix with the dust and dirt from the "grass", and the whole experience began to be very unpleasant to the recruits.

When the whole platoon was involved in incentive training it would usually be brought about due to the platoon doing poorly in some area, usually close order drill, but was not limited to anything in particular. Sometimes we just felt they needed "tightening up" and would put them in to the Pit to accomplish that end. There was a lot to be gained here: for one thing, it was adding conditioning to the recruits over and above normal PT, which we had every day as part of the normal schedule. Ultimately that would pay off when we did our final Physical Fitness Test in which the platoon would be graded as a whole against the other platoons in our series of four platoons. It was secondarily a very good means of getting the platoon to work together, and recognize that they were only as strong as the weakest link. Often, after giving the whole platoon a repetition count of maybe thirty counts of an exercise, we would wait until the count was up to twenty-seven or twenty-eight counts and stop them: "Whoa, stop! Private Smith doesn't want to do the exercises correctly platoon. Come up here Private Smith. Stand in front of the platoon and rest while your platoon does the exercises for you." And with that, Private Smith would have to stand at attention in front of the platoon while the platoon repeated the process. One can only imagine the feelings the platoon were getting for Private Smith. There were sure to be words amongst the recruits at a later time to straighten up Private Smith. That process worked very effectively in getting teamwork into action. It would be repeated on a continuing basis whenever it was needed to accomplish that goal.

Aside from normal physical training exercises that were issued for incentive training, there were also incentive exercises involving the rifle. The rifle used during that era was the M-14 rifle, and it weighed roughly 9 ½ pounds. The rifle was in the possession of recruits while the platoon was conducting close order drill on the parade deck, or other areas where close order drill was practiced. Close order drill was very exacting, and every single movement by the recruits in handling the weapons had to be done precisely in unison with the rest of the platoon, or the whole movement looked very sloppy. The Marine Corps was not known for being sloppy, so that was a critical area for every Marine recruit to master. There were always recruits that could not get these movements down properly. It was very common to bring the whole platoon off the parade deck, and issue incentive training rifle exercises. These would generally consist of taking the M-14 rifle in both hands, and in unison, raise it straight up over the heads for count one, drop it back down to the level of the chest for count two, and then thrust it straight out to the front for count three, and back to the chest for count four. In small numbers that was not difficult. Doing it forty or fifty times was very tiring and tedious, especially if they had to start over before they got to the full count ordered. When I was a recruit that particular drill was one of the most hated and feared because it caused the arms and necks muscles to strain extremely. Worse, recruits still had to carry the rifles back to our areas or continue on with the close order drill that we were called away from, so more time of holding the rifle was coming, and more strain would follow.

If a platoon did poorly at drill, they not only had to deal with the rifle exercises near the parade deck, but would also be put into the Pit when we got back to the area. Sometimes our schedule was very tight, and we would have to give the incentive training later in the day, or that evening during commander's time.

A favorite order of mine when dealing with a belligerent recruit, or one that did poorly was: *"Private, get into the Pit and start doing bends-and-thrusts."* "Sir, how many, sir?" the private would inquire. *"Until the ambulance comes, Maggot!"*

The deeper we got into the training cycle, the more the PT was extended in quantity, and duration. By the time we arrived at the rifle range at Camp Pendleton during the second phase of training the recruits were up to running three miles.

The rifle range had a dirt area across the street from the barracks that was a little over one half mile long, so running three miles was easy to measure, as it was three complete cycles around the dirt area. When a platoon did PT they did so in their boots and utility trousers. Back in those days it was considered proper to wear combat boots to run a three mile run because that was what a Marine would have to do in a combat situation. Today they run in sneakers and PT shorts. Anyone who has run three miles knows how difficult that can be with running shoes. Running those same three miles with combat boots on was a whole different matter altogether!

I would start the platoon on the run by ordering "Double time, march", and off we would go. Running in double time was similar to marching—it required the same precision of movement that marching required. Everyone had to remain in proper alignment back and forth and right-to-left. Each step had to be in unison. Done properly it was poetry in motion. Done incorrectly it looked very sloppy, and needed to be addressed. The first mile of a run was normally without problems. Recruits remained in alignment, and remained in step. Up to that point it was not hard. To keep them tight I would call out that a random private was not in step, and would bring the platoon to a halt and issue incentive training PT. That wore them out a lot more than the run itself. Once the incentive PT was over, we would resume the run, and again, during the second mile, another recruit would be noted for not being in step, or being out of alignment. They would be issued more PT, and that created lots of dust which mixed with their sweat and it created a very uncomfortable feeling. We would soon resume the run. By then the recruits knew that we only have one more loop to complete the three miles. They began to pull together, goading one another to keep it up, and not slip back, get out of step or lose their alignment. The whole time I called out the cadence, and they repeated the cadence calls back. Motivation was setting in. They were now working as a unit. It was time for a little fun! I would work my way toward the front of the platoon during the last quarter mile. Everyone knew where the cutoff was for the three miles, and they were doing everything in their power to stay in perfect formation alignment, keeping in step the whole time. The platoon sounded as one as we ran. I began to sprint ahead of the platoon—they followed, and picked up the pace to stay with me. I went faster. They went faster. I continued, and then would run *past* the three mile mark. It appeared to the recruits that we were going for four miles. Suddenly, there was a visual decline in their gusto—some began to fall back, and the alignment was becoming nonexistent. They were a total mess. They were good in their minds for the three miles, but they gave up when we went beyond that.

Another lesson had to be learned: "*Get in the Pit!*"

SICK BAY COMMANDOS

Recruits were often coddled by their mothers before coming into the Marine Corps. As much as these young men wanted to take on the macho role of being a United States Marine, they often clung to the desire to be coddled when they were not feeling well, or got hurt. Boot camp was going to be a shock to these young men.

We drill instructors had a lot of training we had to accomplish. Everyone must get the same input. Any time a recruit missed a part of training, it slowed down the whole process since a platoon was only as good as its weakest links. We did not coddle recruits, so there was a slight disdain we had for a recruit that wanted to go to sick bay to get treated for an illness or ailment. We expected the recruits to just "suck-it-up", and handle things like a man. However, the SOP called for recruits to be allowed to get medical attention when they needed it.

Each morning after returning from the mess hall, and having completed the morning policing activities in the Quonset huts and the surrounding areas, we would call out: *"Sick bay commandos to the Duty Hut!"* Quonset hut by Quonset hut the squads would repeat the call: "Sir, sick bay commandos to the Duty Hut, aye-aye sir!"

The recruits would line up outside the Duty Hut and one by one they would walk up to the hatch, pound three times on the required spot, and then request permission to enter the Duty Hut. *"I can't hear you"* was the normal response we gave. The process would be repeated several times until finally they were allowed to enter, and then face us at our desk. The private then had to request permission to speak to the drill instructor: "Sir, Private Smith, Platoon 1037, requests permission to speak to the drill instructor, sir!" If the recruit managed to get that part done correctly he would be allowed to speak, otherwise he had to start the whole process over again by stepping outside, and pounding on the hatch again. Once given permission to speak, they would then request to be allowed to go to sick bay. We would start hounding the recruit as to why—there was no doubt in the recruit's mind that it was not something that was going to be granted lightly. I had one recruit that I put through the hatch drill, and after numerous attempts to get the procedure down, finally stated that he wanted to go to sick bay to get checked because he thought he had crabs. I asked: *"Numb Nuts, how the hell would you know if you have crabs? Are you a doctor, Dipshit?"* The recruit responded with: "Sir, the private just thinks he has crabs, sir." I was not going to let it go at that so I gave the following order: *"Private Crabs, you go back to your hut and catch a crab and bring it to me as proof you have them! Get out of my office right now!"* He turned, and ran out of the Duty Hut, shocked that he was treated so harshly. I turned my attention to the next recruit, and continued with the short line that had formed. Finally, the crab-case was back at my hatch, pounding on it, and requesting permission to enter. After a serious round of attempts, he finally was granted permission to enter, and finally to speak: "Sir, the private caught a crab, sir." At that he thrust out his hand and, sure enough, there was a small insect-like creature in his palm. I gave him permission to go to sick bay.

Recruits knew that if they missed enough training it could result in their being set back in training into another platoon to start over, or to pick up where they needed to catch up, so they were not motivated to gold-brick (the act of faking illness to avoid work or training). Often the medical officers, or a corpsman, would give the recruit either a "light duty chit" or a "bed-rest chit". Light duty meant that the recruit could not participate in heavy activity such as PT, close order drill or the obstacle course—even incentive training was not in the cards. Bed rest was given to recruits that had serious illness, such as the flu, or significant fevers. Light duty and bed rest were only granted for short periods of time, and often required that the recruit be sent back for another evaluation by the medical officer, or corpsman, before being allowed to resume normal training.

Some of the most common ailments to recruits were injuries to their feet. Heel contusions were bruises on the heel that were caused by the recruit not properly setting his foot down while marching. After repeated poundings to the deck, the heel of the foot becomes very tender, and eventually will totally debilitate a recruit, and prevent him from marching or doing physical training. A recruit with heel contusions would need to rest his foot for several days, soak the foot in hot water at night, and also be required to wear his tennis shoes instead of his boots. Blisters were another foot issue that was common. Some of the recruits were really "tenderfeet" in the truest sense of the word. Sometimes it was necessary for a recruit to be re-issued another pair of boots that fit better. Blisters left untreated could become infected and lead to serious medical problems. Every night the recruits would be inspected by us to ensure they did not have issues, or that they were treating their ailments correctly.

The close quarters that the recruits lived in, and the proximity to so many people from different parts of the country. They were exposed to many new germs and illnesses that they had not developed immunities for. The first couple of weeks of training were the most likely time recruits would come down with these ailments. The recruits quickly discovered what ailments we were going to acknowledge as worthy of going to sick bay, and those that were not. A case of the "sniffles" or a "headache" was not going to be treated with a lot of sympathy from us.

All heavy recruit activities such as running the obstacle course, group physical training, extended runs, etc, required that the series be accompanied by a military ambulance that had two corpsmen riding in it. They were always prepared to treat an injury immediately, or to haul a recruit off to the medical facilities for further treatment if needed. Occasionally a recruit would fall from an obstacle, and break an arm or leg. During hot weather it was not uncommon for a recruit to come down with heat exhaustion, or even suffer heat stroke. Those cases were tended to immediately, and without any delays.

As leaders, we had to live by what they said and did. We also had ailments, but we had to show the recruits that being a Marine meant being tough, so we just continued on, and gutted it out. As drill instructors, we were *never* "sick bay commandos".

DISTRACTIONS BY PROXIMITY

The Marine Corps Recruit Depot in San Diego offers the same training format as does their counterpart at Parris Island, South Carolina. San Diego has several major advantages over Parris Island: it has really great weather, and there are no sand fleas, or alligators.

There are also distinct disadvantages at San Diego that Parris Island does not have to deal with: MCRD, San Diego, is located adjacent to Lindbergh Field, San Diego's primary airport, and they are right in the hub of downtown San Diego.

Recruits can see the surrounding city sights while at MCRD. That can create a homesick feeling in some recruits, as they were constantly reminded of the outside world. Parris Island was literally an island, and had no views of towns, homes or anything that the recruits could identify with to make them homesick, or distracted. It was extremely difficult for a recruit to go AWOL (Absent without leave) at Parris Island. Parris Island was surrounded by the alligator-infested waters. Since San Diego did not have alligators, and water surrounding it, the result was more recruits "jumping the fence" (going absent without leave). We used to attempt to discourage the recruits from even thinking about jumping the fence, and running across the runways, by telling them that one or two recruits per month had to be scraped off the runways because they could not beat the jets that were landing, or taking off. Recruits could disappear quickly in the city surroundings if they chose to run away. The recruits at Parris Island did not have that option, at least so easily available to them.

The proximity of Lindbergh Field to MCRD created a noise nuisance that was constant. During the Vietnam era, there were no limitations on when flights arrived, or left Lindbergh Field. There also were no noise restrictions then, so the jet engine noise was considerably louder back then than they allow with the standards of today. Jets landed, or took off, every few minutes, twenty-four hours per day, and seven days per week. Every time a jet would land it would turn on its thrust-reversers to slow their ground speed, and that created a shrilly howl that was deafening. Trying to sleep with that racket going on was very difficult. There was also the constant smell of jet fumes and exhaust that filled the air.

We had to learn to use a "jet pause" when speaking to the recruits: every time a jet took off the extremely loud roar made it impossible for us to be heard, so the we had to pause long enough for the jet to move on before continuing. That made the close order drill very difficult, as drill was a precision movement, and it was sometimes not possible to pause while the jet roared by when giving commands for the drill movements. Recruits somehow tuned in to our voices, and could discern them over the roar of the jets. However, when they couldn't hear us, the results were a disaster to the drill movement!

Every time a jet took off, the recruits could also picture themselves on the plane going home. The jets were distracting to everyone that was within eye-sight, or hearing distance. It did not take us long to discourage the recruits from watching the planes: as soon as the we caught a recruit eyeballing the jet's movements we would immediately start yelling at the recruit to keep his head, and eyes, straight ahead. A little incentive PT helped cure the problem as well.

As soon as the series would move to the rifle range at Edson Range, for the second phase of training, the jets, and their distractions, were behind us. However, the barracks at Edson Range were located next to Interstate 5, and we then had to contend with the roar of the traffic blasting by at seventy to eighty miles per hour. That noise was also constant throughout the day, and night. It was much easier for a recruit to go AWOL (absent without leave) at Edson Range due to the base being more remote then MCRD was. The sights and sounds of cars traveling up and down the freeway was another distraction that caused recruits to get homesick.

By the time the recruits returned to MCRD for completion of third phase, they had pretty well dialed in our voices so that, even with the roar of a jet taking off or landing, they would hear the commands we gave them. The jets were still loud and annoying, but by then, were a lesser distraction.

At least MCRD, San Diego, did not have to deal with alligators and sand fleas that Parris Island had.

MAIL CALL

Recruits, upon getting assigned to a platoon, were ordered to send a letter home to their family to advise them that they arrived at boot camp, and to give them their new military address. The recruits were also told to advise their family to *not send any* contraband, or things like cookies or candy.

The atmosphere the recruits were under broke their spirits very easily. After all, that was one of the purposes of boot camp: break them down so that they could be rebuilt in the Marine Corps mold. The first couple of weeks were the absolute worst for the recruits, as they were in a daze most of the time, and under complete duress from the moment they woke up, till the moment they finally got to sleep that night.

Usually, by the end of the first or second week, mail began to arrive for the recruits. One of the most looked-forward to events of the recruit day was "mail call", the time we passed out mail. Usually, around 1930 to 1945 (7:30 PM to 7:45 PM), which was just prior to recruit free time, we would call out: "*On the road in mail call formation.*" The call then was repeated by each squad in the Quonset huts: "Sir, on the road in mail call formation, aye-aye sir!" They then ran outside on the road, and stood in two columns while three recruits brought their foot lockers to stack up in the middle of the road. At that point we would walk up to the stack of footlockers, treating them as a podium. We would start at the top of the mail stack and call out the recruit to whom the letter was addressed. The recruit would run up and accept his letter. The process was repeated until all the mail was delivered. They were not allowed to read their mail before free time. Once all the mail was delivered the recruits would be put on free time which was the one hour they were allotted each day to read and write mail, polish their boots, and get prepared for the next days' training.

Nothing in boot camp can compare to a letter from home. The look on the face of a recruit receiving a letter told the story: they were elated. Their spirits went up immediately. They couldn't wait to hear from a friend, or family member. It eased their anxieties for the moment. There were some recruits that received a lot of mail. Then, there were some recruits that did not get any mail. Those recruits that did not get mail I always felt sorry for. It was apparent that they felt very lost without contact from the outside world. Maybe they didn't have anyone who cared. There were recruits that you could see the wind visibly come out of them when mail call was over, and they did not get a letter and it was very disheartening for them.

One of the functions we had at mail call was to detect contraband. When passing out the mail we felt each envelope to determine if there was anything inside that felt like something other than a letter. When there was something suspicious inside, the recruit would be ordered to open it in front of us. During that era it was entirely likely that a friend of the recruit might think it would be a great idea to send a marijuana joint, or some other drug of choice, to their pal in boot camp. That would be a big problem for the recruit if we found contraband. Contraband of that nature had to be reported. In addition, the recruit was going to pay heavily for his pal's indiscretion—usually endless periods in the Pit doing incentive PT.

Contraband was not just drugs—it could be chewing gum, candy, or other items that were restricted. Pogey bait (sweets, candy, etc) was the most common type of contraband received. The recruits always had to spend time in the Pit for receiving contraband—although it was not their direct fault that a friend, or family member sent the contraband, the recruits were supposed to have notified them in their first letter that they could not receive any contraband, and to *not* send it.

Girl friends of the recruits could sometimes be their worst enemy without knowing it. Girls loved to spray a little perfume on their letters before sending them off to their boyfriends. Sometimes they would write mushy things on the outside of the envelopes. Some girls would kiss the envelope leaving an impression of their lips with their lipstick. These doctored letters drew a large amount of *negative attention* from us toward the recruit when the letter was delivered. The recruit would be told in no uncertain terms that they would have to write back and emphatically advise these girl friends of the predicaments they put the recruit in when they received them. Within a short period of time the problem would usually go away.

Mothers of the recruits always wanted to bake cookies, and send them to their little darlings to cheer them up. They had no idea of the catastrophic result that was going to bring to their son. When a box arrived the recruit was called up during mail call and told to open the package. He would then be required to eat the entire contents while he was standing there. If he was lucky the contents were only a small amount of cookies or brownies. If he was not, and the package contained candy bars, chewing gum or similar packaged goods, he would have to eat the whole package—that meant wrappers and all! On top of that, once they were done they were sent to the Pit for a little incentive training, followed by another stern warning to write home and advise the family to *not send any more goodies!*

The most devastating letter a recruit could receive was the "Dear John" letter. They were inevitable. The girl back home would decide to move on, and cut the ties. The recruit was having a hard enough time coping with his new life in the Marine Corps, and then his girl friend dumped him—that was totally devastating to the recruit.

There were some occasions in which the recruit would receive news that did not come in the mail—we would receive a telegram from the Red Cross saying that a family member had died or suffered some life-threatening crisis. I was the duty NCO one night while at Edson Range. The Red Cross sent a telegram that came to me, notifying us that the father of one of the recruits in my platoon had just had a major heart attack, and he was not expected to make it. The recruit was going to be given emergency leave, and would be immediately sent back to MCRD, San Diego, where he would be issued a dress uniform, and put on a plane home to deal with the crisis. My job was to call the recruit to the office and break the news to him, and then have him go pack his gear. When the recruit arrived I said: "Private, we have just received some very bad news: your father just had a heart attack, and he is not expected to make it. You are being …" Before I could finish my words the recruit broke down, and started to cry like a baby. I had never encountered a situation like this as a drill instructor. I understood his grief, but this was the Marine Corps. Acting instinctively I jumped up out of my chair, knocking the chair over backwards, and leaned over the desk toward the recruit and yelled: *"Private, Marines don't cry! Stand up straight, and compose yourself right now. You are being sent home on emergency leave, and you need to go back to the squad bay, and pack all your gear. You are going back to MCRD tonight to be issued a dress uniform so you can fly home. Do you understand me?"* At that the recruit snapped to attention, wiped away the tears and said "Sir, yes sir!" I never saw this recruit again, but I know in my heart that moment was a turning point in the maturity of the recruit: he went from being a sniffling boy, to being a man in the blink-of-an-eye.

CLOSE ORDER DRILL

Close order drill was one of the fundamental subjects taught to Marine recruits. It was probably the highest form of discipline training that a recruit went through while in boot camp. That training started the minute the recruit stepped off the bus and his feet landed on the yellow footprints.

Close order drill requires precise motions and crisp actions. Each movement was going to be practiced over, and over again. The platoons were going to be rated on how well they performed drill movements on two occasions during the training cycles: once in the first phase, called "Initial Drill", and then again in the third phase called, "Final Drill". The four platoons in the recruit series were going to be graded at those events, and the platoon that got the highest score was going to be the victor in the series' competition. In the Marine Corps, every unit has a Guideon that is a pole with the platoon flag, with its identifying number, or unit number, on it, and it is carried by the Platoon Guide who stands at the front of the platoon. The winning platoon was going to get a pennant that would hang from the platoon Gideon, and it would remain there for the remaining duration of training. It was a great honor to be the best at the drill competitions.

The Drill Instructor School spent more time in teaching the drill instructor candidates close order drill than any other subject. Every nuance of each drill movement had to be memorized by us, and we had to be able to articulate to the recruits, every single nuance of the movements. We also had to be able to demonstrate each movement to the recruits, and get them to comprehend exactly what was required.

The "manual of arms" are the movements that involve the rifle. The rifle must be carried by the recruits, and there are six separate rifle movements. Marching movements were hard enough, but the manual of arms while marching were even more difficult to master, as there were many things involved each time the rifle was moved from one position to another.

Drill was my personal favorite subject in all of my experiences as a drill instructor. It was the most immediately gratifying of the subjects that we taught.

We could tell right away whether it was being done correctly or not: in most cases at the beginning it was not.

Two drill instructors had to be present at a minimum on the daily two hours spent on the parade deck teaching drill. Our eyes were always looking for any recruit that missed a beat, or was using an incorrect motion, or movement. We were quick to correct a recruit if he screwed up. When we would get into the face of one recruit, and bellow out our dissatisfaction with his actions, all those around him got the same message. Absolutely none of them wanted to be singled out. The fact was, at some point, they were all singled out. The recruits practiced repetition after repetition of each movement. There were countless miles of marching up, and down, the parade deck.

The parade deck in San Diego is the largest parade deck of any facility in the Marine Corps. It is almost one half of a mile long, and about 500 feet wide. It seemed larger when you were on it, and even longer still if you were a recruit holding a 9 ½ pound M-14 rifle. The parade deck got extremely warm in the summer months. It felt like your boot soles were melting into the asphalt when we were standing on it. In the winter, as mild as the climate was in San Diego, the deck seemed like it was made from ice—feet got numb from the cold coming through. But, hot or cold, every day the recruits spent two hours on the parade deck. We referred to the parade deck as "the Grinder".

The Grinder had lots of traffic during the Vietnam era due to the many thousands of recruits that were going through boot camp. Recruit battalions had at least one recruit series on the Grinder at any one time. That meant there was a total of 12 platoons moving up and down the Grinder. It took a lot of care to not crash a platoon into another platoon.

The trip to, and from the Grinder was generally a march of about a quarter of a mile, or more, and every foot of it was used as additional practice time. In addition, movements were practiced on every trip to the mess hall, classrooms, and any other place we had to march the platoons to. Drill was on-going.

Anyone who watched TV in the late 1960's saw the program "Gomer Pyle". It was a show about a goofy Marine recruit and his drill instructor Gunnery Sergeant Carter, and the show was based at MCRD, San Diego. It fairly well depicted an accurate vision of the scenery of the base, but Gomer Pyle himself was hardly what a typical recruit was like. Gomer was constantly screwing something up, to the chagrin of his DI, Gunnery Sergeant Carter. The problem was, every platoon ended up with a recruit like Gomer Pyle. That recruit was someone that was always getting the drill movement wrong. No matter how much time was spent trying to teach him the correct way, and no matter how much we got into his face, he inevitably *still* got something wrong. A "Gomer Pyle" in the platoon was something that could drive a sane DI insane. *"Why are you torturing me, private?"*

In the third week of First Phase, platoons went out for Initial Drill Evaluations. That was big. The platoon was competing for bragging rights. The senior-most of the two junior drill instructors in each platoon was usually selected to take the platoon out for the drill evaluation. The drill instructors were going to be rated for their abilities of teaching the recruits close order drill. The evaluation was a series of about twenty-five to thirty drill movements, including the manual of arms. The movements were based on a card the drill instructor had been given by the evaluators. The evaluators were senior Staff NCOs from the Recruit Training Regiment, and the instructors of the Drill Instructor School. They knew exactly what to look for, and nothing was going to get past them. Not only was the platoon going to be evaluated for how well they performed the movements on the cards, but also how well the drill instructor conducted himself in commanding the platoon. A poor performance by the DI could ruin the chances of winning the pennant, and the DI stood a chance of being reprimanded himself.

The evaluators were looking for little things: the recruits' eyes following the drill instructor instead of looking straight ahead; feet at a 45 degree angle in the position of attention; a head moving slightly when the rifle was moved from one shoulder to the other. It was generally the little things that made the biggest difference in the final score. They even counted the steps-per-minute to make sure the drill instructors' cadence was exactly 120 steps each minute. We was going to be judged on how clearly our commands were given; the volume in our voice, as well as the inflections used; our military bearing, and even our appearance— absolutely nothing was going to escape these guys. The drill instructor conducting the drill evaluation was going to spend hours making his uniform as perfect as possible. Commands were going to be rehearsed for hours in addition to the regular duties the drill instructor faces daily.

One of the things that potentially was a problem in the drill evaluations was "Gomer Pyle", the platoon idiot, who could never get the movements right. On the morning of Initial Drill or Final Drill, "Gomer" was usually sent to sick bay so that he was not available to march in the contest. A record of where all recruits who were not present had to be provided to the evaluators prior to the evaluation in order to account for the platoons' total. The evaluators were wise to the tricks of our trade. If too many recruits were absent based on the normal count, it could affect the score.

When it was all done and said, one of the four platoons was going to take the honors, and that platoon would become euphoric upon learning of their victory. It was good for a lot of motivational milege, and was a big thrust for that platoon as they moved into Second Phase at the rifle range.

Final Drill was basically the same thing as Initial Drill. The primary difference was that this evaluation was done in Third Phase, and consisted of many more movements that had been learned since Initial Drill in First Phase. That competition was almost always conducted by the Platoon Commander. The evaluation was one of the last events scheduled for the platoon, and it was going to be one of the "last hurrahs" for the platoon that took the competition, and got the pennant. All of the drill instructor's skills, actions, and lessons were now going to unfold as a score. That was also going to be a victory for the winning Platoon Commander for bragging rights as the best Platoon Commander in the series.

A platoon that did not do well in drill competitions was going to pay a price after it was done. They were going to spend considerable time in the Pit, and they were not going to like the losing side of it. We were going to be all over them. In the case of Final Drill, it was not going to matter that they would be graduating soon—they were going to pay for being inept. Of course they knew this going into it in the beginning, so they generally were going to push themselves to their limits to do well. Still, like all competitions, there was only *one* winner.

My keen interest in drill drove me to excel at both teaching it, and conducting it. I spent every spare minute allotted during "Commanders Time", which was the time we had to teach subjects that we felt that the platoon needed additional work in, and usually amounted to one to two extra hours each day working on drill. I was a fanatic on drill. I demanded excellence, and the lack of it resulted in lots of additional incentive training in the Pit.

I was always the most junior drill instructor in a series due to my short time in the Marine Corps, and time on the drill field, so I was usually not the one that was selected to take the platoon out for Initial Drill. More and more I was building confidence from my Platoon Commander, as to my abilities, and my efforts finally paid off in a big way. My Platoon Commander, Staff Sergeant Able, had been going to the dental department for a series of oral surgeries during the same time-frame as our Final Drill was scheduled. He was not going to be able to effectively give the commands at the drill that would be good enough to even remotely stand a chance to win the contest. He had been impressed with my handling of the drill with the platoon, so he gave me the nod to do the Final Drill. That was an extremely big honor for me personally, and I was the only junior drill instructor in the event. The platoons go out in the sequence of their platoon numbers, and we had the last number in the series, so we went last at the evaluation. That made it a little unnerving because the other platoon scores were already known at the time our platoon went out, and the pressure was really on—way more pressure than the other platoons had because we knew what we were up against. I was very nervous. All the seniors' eyes were on me, including the Company Commander and Battalion Commander, who viewed the event as spectators. That was also my very first drill evaluation. I reported to the evaluators, and drew my card from a random stack. It was "show time".

"FALL IN" I commanded from a position of attention while standing in the middle of the Grinder. Immediately, eighty-five recruits ran from the edge of the Grinder to form platoon formation, centered directly in front of me. My mind was racing while thinking about every possible fear of things that could go wrong. I looked over the formation to make sure they were in alignment and properly covered front-to-back. I looked at the first movement on the card and slowly composed myself. I wanted to make sure that I was thinking through the process so that I could keep my cool, and not make an error. Each movement completed would require the approval of the evaluators before proceeding—they needed time to scan the platoon, and jot down notes. They gave the nod to proceed. I looked at the card, and saw that the first movement was a Right Face. "Right, Face" I commanded loudly, and with the proper inflection on the word "right". The platoon sharply executed the movement. All recruits were in unison. All heels came together at the same time. So far, so good. We continued down the card, and I would give the next command at the nod of the evaluators. One at a time, we went through each movement, including the manual of arms, while the platoon remained stationary. I was getting comfortable with it, and made sure I was slow and deliberate in my delivery. I knew that the hardest part would be the marching movements, as I would not be issuing the commands directly in front of the platoon, instead, I would be along the side of the platoon, and my voice would be more difficult to be heard in the front. Marching movements were also a little more difficult because more things were happening at the same time: cadence was being called, front and rear alignment had to be maintained, and there were specific pivot points recruits had to step on when the platoon was given a turning movement. Plus, the manual of arms was going to be executed on the march, and that meant that the rifles were going to be shifted from one shoulder to another all while still maintaining the proper cadence, alignment, etc. It was a little scary to me as we moved, as I was aware of the evaluators walking along side, counting the steps per minute; checking on the alignment and cover; looking for elbows out of position, heads nodding on rifle movements, etc. But things were looking good to me. In my mind my platoon was doing well. I was confident about my own actions too. But, the final score was not going to be based on what I thought, but rather what the evaluators thought. I also kept in mind I was a junior drill instructor, and not a Platoon Commander, so I was bucking the tradition of the game here, and I knew the other Platoon Commanders resented my handling of that drill evaluation. I was wondering if the evaluators might see it that way too. So many things were going through my mind, as I continued to go through the movements on the card. Finally I reached the end. With a nod from the evaluator, I issued the order "Fallout", and the platoon ran to the edge of the Grinder, and fell back into platoon formation and awaited the results.

The evaluators took their time in tallying their results. They then needed to compare their evaluations, and average out the results. It seemed like an eternity. They finally finished, and approached me to review their findings. They informed me that they were blown away by my performance! I had outdone the other Platoon Commanders by a wide margin. In fact, the margin was so much higher that the Platoon Commanders were actually embarrassed by their much lower scores. I came as close to acing the competition with a perfect score as one could get. They congratulated me on a superior performance in both my delivery, and presentation, and also by my command presence, and military bearing. It doesn't get any better than that! Or so I thought. The next day I received a Letter of Commendation from the Battalion Commander, Lieutenant Colonel Sutter, for my excellent performance. He noted that I had done a superior job with far less experience than those with whom I competed. At that point, I knew I had arrived as a capable drill instructor, and my career was going to zoom going forward.

SPECIAL TRAINING BRANCH

Once a recruit got assigned to a platoon, he became fixated on staying with that platoon the entire time he was in boot camp. Nothing in his mind could be worse than being set back in training, and going to another platoon. No matter how harsh we were, nor how bad he perceived things to be where he currently was at, being set back in training was believed by the recruit, to be the worse possible thing that could happen to him. The reality was that about 1/3 of the recruits were going to be set back for a variety of reasons. Most of the recruits were set back for medical reasons—they got banged up in training, and needed time to recover. Some needed additional time to develop their physical conditioning, as they could not keep up. Some had some severe attitude issues, and needed a little motivating that went above the normal. Then there were the violators of the rules, the ones that needed a little "jail" time to learn how to cope. Whatever the problem was, the Marines had a solution—it was called the "Special Training Branch" (STB).

STB was a great tool for us. The recruits learned very early after their arrival about STB, and it drew the fear of death into them to think they could be sent there. In fact, they would probably rather be sent to the Siberian salt mines than be sent to Special Training Branch training. In addition to having to transfer into a strange platoon at a later date, they often had to start over in a training cycle they had already gone through. Extending boot camp was not a pleasant thought to anyone.

We did not like getting transfers in from STB either. Once they had completed their assignment at STB, the recruits were reassigned to another platoon. They came in with "salty" attitudes, and they often had a negative impact on the regulars in the platoon. We called them "Shitbirds". We often went out of our ways to make sure the Shitbirds knew *who* was in charge.

Medical Rehabilitation Platoon (MRP) was the most often used platoon at STB. That was where recruits were sent after they were deemed in need of medical rehabilitation by the medical staff. Recruits often got fractures, heel contusions, ailments, and strains that kept them from keeping up with their platoons while rehabilitating. They would spend their days getting classroom instructions on various subjects, and upon their release; they often came back very much ahead of the other recruits in terms of their military knowledge. It was sometimes comical to watch the MRP march to the mess hall, as most were either on crutches, or had arms in slings, and they looked really rag-tag. Their stay in MRP was dependent on their ailment, and only the medical officers could determine when they were ready to go back into regular training.

Physical Training Platoon (PCP) was for the physically unfit recruits. During the Vietnam conflict the services were forced to take what was called a "Category Four" recruit, who would not have been accepted had there not been due to the war effort. These recruits were often extremely overweight or underweight and most were totally unfit physically. Most could not pass the initial physical fitness testing conducted when the recruits initially start training. So, they were sent to PCP for conditioning. PCP was often referred to as the "Fat Farm" by us. Those recruits were usually put on diets—the skinny ones had to eat more, and the fat ones were restricted to lettuce and vegetables. They spent the vast majority of their days doing physical training of all types to get them into shape. Their stay in PCP was totally dependent on the recruit's ability to pass a minimum physical fitness test. Some spent a long time in PCP. When they were finally sent to a new platoon for continuing their training they were not accepted well by either the recruits or us. They were usually sub-par still, and they were going to have a negative impact on the platoon's progress in physical areas. In many cases these recruits were still unable to complete training with their newly assigned platoons, having to be sent back again.

There were some recruits that were unable to read when they arrived. Or they were mentally slow, with low IQ's. It was really hard to believe that here in America there would be kids that could not read, but they showed up in the Marine Corps. That was really a sad statement as to the state of affairs with our nation during the Vietnam War—we had to accept people for training that could not read. One might think that reading was not needed for many of the war ventures, but that was totally not true. If a Marine could not read he couldn't tell what type of ammo was in the ammo box. He couldn't read basic instructions, or orders. Those recruits were assigned to Academic Instruction Platoon (AIP). They were given special tutorial instruction on reading, and other areas they needed special assistance with. Until they had developed enough to move forward they stayed in that platoon. Some of them never were able to achieve the needed academic proficiency, and were discharged and sent home. Quite a number of them made it through, and went into regular training. I always admired their tenacity, but they were going to need special attention all the way through boot camp.

Recruits must adhere to the Uniform Code of Military Justice (UCMJ). Anyone violating the rules was subject to court martial and potential brig time. Recruit training had a simple system for the rule violators. Once they were caught committing a violation, they were sent to the Company Commander for "Office Hours". That was where the Company Commander listened to the case, and then rendered a sentence. That sentence could be anywhere from one to two weeks in Correctional Custody Platoon (CCP). In CCP they spent their days doing hard labor—*very hard labor*. They were often seen marching to and from a rock pile with sledge hammers, picks, and shovels instead of M-14 rifles. They had to carry two buckets at a time in addition to their tools. They were also required to wear a silver colored metal helmet, and their blouses had CCP on them. The drill instructors that were in charge of those recruits had a field day with them in terms of being tough on them. They would march them to the rock pile, and then the recruit would spend all day breaking big rocks into little rocks. When they were not crushing rocks they were digging holes. They had to carry their buckets with dirt or rocks piled in them to the hilt. Their stay in CCP was designed to be similar to a regular brig. Any recruit that came back to regular training from CCP was a valuable source of passing the word to the regulars in the platoon as to just how bad life can be if you violate the rules. One of two things would happen with those recruits: either they came back, and turned a corner, and went on to productive careers, or they were still "Joe Willie Switchblade", and would soon either be back in CCP, or out of the Marine Corps.

The absolute best tool available in STB was "Motivation Platoon "(MP). Recruit training could create a lot of stress for recruits, and many arrived at MCRD under a very naïve understanding of what they were in for. Many had never been under a disciplined environment in their lives, and were accustomed to doing whatever they wanted. They had sassed their mothers when asked to clean their rooms; were belligerent to authority figures, such as teachers and police. The whole atmosphere of the 1960's, and early 1970's, was one of rebellion for youths that comprised the Baby Boomers. I often wondered what possessed some of these recruits to enlist in the Marines in the first place—it wasn't like our training methods were a secret. They should have known what they were getting into. Sadly, that was not always the case. Some of these young men needed a little more coaching than the rest. If a recruit refused to obey our commands, or was belligerent to us he was going to be recommended to be assigned to the Motivation Platoon. That was probably the absolute *worst place* any recruit would want to end up at.

Motivation Platoon had a special set of Standard Operating Procedures (SOP) than normal recruit training had. It was much more liberal, and the tactics they could use to motivate a recruit could be considered "over the top" when compared to regular SOP rules for standard training situations. Motivation Platoon DI's were all over the recruits. First off, they had more DI's assigned to those platoons than a standard platoon, so the recruits got more "special attention" than normal. Absolutely nothing got past those DI's. Recruits were given incentive training at the drop of a hat. The DI's could be more physical with the recruits also. They were allowed to create a living hell for these young, belligerent recruits. They had special techniques they could use for extreme cases—one example was being able to have a recruit strip naked, and then be handcuffed to a full-length mirror for extended periods of time. That technique caused the recruit to have to look at himself in the mirror. It may not seem like much, but when they were doing that all day long, and having a little extra yelling, and screaming in their ears from the MP DI's, they started to see themselves a little differently than when they were first put there. They started to realize they were not Superman, but only a frail looking wimpy person—the person they really were. In most cases, after spending one or two weeks in Motivation Platoon were enough to straighten out even the most hardened cases. At that point the recruit was assigned back to training with a new platoon. Those recruits were often not liked at all by us since they had already shown themselves to be problems in their previous platoons. But we did not have a choice, and had to take them.

The Motivation Platoon no longer exists in the Marine Corps. Sometime during the 1980's a recruit in Motivation Platoon was undergoing special training with Pugil Sticks. Pugil sticks are heavy poles about six feet long that have heavy padding on both ends and padded hand-guards in the middle. They were used to simulate rifle and bayonet hand-to-hand combat. Recruits engage in that simulation by attempting to hit another recruit who was also equipped with a pugil stick. Recruits were required to wear a football helmet during those matches to protect them from the blows. In most cases in regular recruit training the recruits rotate through a round-robin match, attempting to give a "killing blow" to their opponent in order to move forward in the match. On that particular day the recruit from Motivation Platoon was not acting with enough gusto to satisfy his DI's, and they kept him in the ring to face opponent after opponent in an effort to get him to fight with enthusiasm. He was not responding well enough, and they kept putting in fresh recruits to clobber him. Eventually he took enough blows to the head, that despite the helmet he wore, caused severe brain damage, and the recruit died. That was truly unfortunate. It created quite an uproar with the local newspapers creating significant negative press about those training tactics. There was a major investigation of the events, and Marine Corps training once again came under close scrutiny. The DI's were acting within their expanded SOP. The Marine Corps ultimately decided that the Motivation Platoon was something that was not needed. The recruits that did not truly want to be in the Marines were no longer going to be forced to accept it: they would simply be sent home. That was a radical change from the previous policy of once they signed up and gave their oath, they were in the service until the end of their enlistment. At first hearing of the changes I was surprised that the Marines would do away with such a powerful motivation tool, but on second thought, I agree that the change was for the better. After all, a problem recruit ultimately turns out to be a problem Marine, and the Marine Corps does not have room for problem Marines.

PARADES

Training during the Vietnam era involved a lot of pomp and ceremony. It was deemed that recruits would be involved in two parades while in training. The purpose of that was to instill a sense of the regalia of military ceremonies, and to promote teamwork. Teamwork was essential in a parade as every platoon must be in step with, and in line with all the others. The parades also served another purpose during that era: Marines returning from Vietnam who were awarded medals for valor would be presented those medals during the parade ceremonies. That furthered the sense of what the Marines were all about.

The parade would consist of recruits from both the First Phase and Final Phase. There was a series from a battalion for both phases, for a total of two recruit series totaling eight platoons. Those parades were huge, consisting of over 700 recruits. The parades would be held every Friday, and each week a different battalion held the parade. For the recruits in First Phase, it would be the first time they marched to the drum-beat of a marching band.

Parades took a while to stage. First, the platoons had to arrive at the staging area which was located at the south end of the parade deck. Like most things in training, they hurried up to get there, and then they waited. The Final Phase recruits were set up in the front, and the First Phase in the rear. Once the platoons were staged, they were given the command of "Parade Rest" so that they were not standing with locked legs for extended periods that could result in recruits fainting. However, parades held in the summer months were in the heat of the day, and no matter how much care was taken to prevent stress, there were always some recruits that fainted from the extended standing and heat. The medical corps was always present with their gray ambulances to take recruits to sick bay if they dropped.

Parades were normally called "officer parades" due to the parade staff being made up primarily of officers. In most standard parades throughout the Marine Corps that was how the staffing was normally structured. The Commander of Troops was an officer, and he had a staff of mostly officers. However, there would always be an assignment of NCOs made up of drill instructors, which also were part of the officer's staff. We were often called upon to attend those parades on our days off. There would also be practices for the parades which took a lot of additional time from the little time we had to spare.

After the officer staff positioned themselves in the center of the parade deck, the officer who started the parade by his commands, the Parade Adjutant, would smartly march to the north end of the parade deck near where the band was staged. The band would sound "Adjutants Call", and then the adjutant would yell out the order "Attention" to the troops. That was a difficult task—the distance involved was considerable, and his voice had to carry to the very last person in the staging area. The adjutants' voice was competing with both the noise of the airplanes departing, and landing, at Lindbergh field that was adjacent to MCRD, as well as having to deal with the natural noise of the wind that blew across the parade deck. The battalion snaps to the position of attention. The adjutant next gave the order "Forward, march", and the parade was on. The platoons marched straight down the field to the beat of the band, and upon hitting a predetermined spot, would stop, and begin marching in place at the command of "Mark time, march" until the platoons were in position. They then halted and did a facing movement so that all platoons were facing the west side of the parade deck toward the reviewing stand. At that point the colors would be marched onto the field, and the national anthem would be played by the band. The next order from the Adjutant was "Sound off", and all units would report that all personnel were present or accounted for. The adjutant would then march smartly to the officer staff, and gave the report to the Commander of Troops. The adjutant would then read the Publication of Orders, and call Officers Center in which all the platoon commanders would march to the center of the formation, and then proceed in formation to the Commander of Troops. The formation saluted the officers, and then returned to their platoons.

At that point in the parades there would be a presentation of the awards for valor, and those Marines getting decorations would be individually cited for their actions, and presented their medals. When that was completed the parade was ready to commence again. The adjutant would then call out: "Pass in Review". At that the parade would begin again. Platoons were given the order "Forward, March", and off they went, marching to the sound of marching music. The platoons would turn left twice at predetermined points on the parade deck, and would soon pass directly in front of the Reviewing Stand where the Reviewing Officer and his guests stood. Also present were the Marines who were presented medals. As each platoon passed the reviewing officer, their platoon commanders ordered "Eyes, Right", and the three left squads turned their heads to the right, the squad on the right side continued to look straight ahead to keep the alignment correct. The Reviewing Officer returned their salutes. At that point the parade would be over for each platoon, and they would continue marching back to their areas.

I always liked the parades—it was the only chance we had to march to marching music, and that added a new dimension to what I already felt was the best part of being a drill instructor. Other than the fact that our platoons had to stand at the position of attention for long periods of time, as well as to carry their weapons for an eternity, the recruits also liked the pomp and ceremony.

The Commanding General decided he wanted to re-introduce a "Noncommissioned Officer Parade" to the procedures. Everything was basically the same as the Officer Parade, but the staff would be made of up of all NCOs with no officers. As usual, with my junior-man status, I was selected for the first NCO parade. I checked out my NCO sword at the equipment room, and reported for the practice. They "volunteered" me to be the Adjutant. As the Adjutant I would somehow have to get my voice to carry almost a quarter of a mile, over and above the roar of airplanes and wind noise, and yet still be heard. That was a tall order for a little guy like me! One thing that would be a little different from the Officer Parades—we drill instructors were used to giving commands, and marching troops, whereas the officers were not. That gave us an edge in the voice commands needed, and the execution of the sword manual of arms we were required to perform. So we practiced and practiced. That would be a biggy as far as we were concerned—they had not had an NCO parade in more than twenty years, and it was going to be viewed by the Commanding General, and his staff.

Our parade ended up going without a single hitch or snag. I was able to loudly and clearly give all the commands and the execution was superb by the platoons. Not a single beat was missed. It was definitely a success. A few days after the parade I received a Letter of Commendation from the Commanding General noting the excellence of my delivery, and the success of the parade. That was quite an achievement for me, and I was very proud of how well it went.

There were some occasions in which a recruit series was ordered to participate in a local parade outside of the base. Those were always a treat for the recruits, as they were able to leave the stresses of the boot camp environment at MCRD, and take in some of the local San Diego flavor. There were marching bands that were always motivating to hear, and the recruits always delighted in the close proximity to the many girls that participate in the parades from the local high schools and colleges. The series that were selected to participate in these parades were always series that were in the Final Phase of training, as they marched the best and looked the sharpest—image was everything!

THE RIFLE RANGE

The second phase of training took place at the rifle range, and that required relocating to Camp Pendleton about 45 miles north along the Pacific coastline. The recruit series had to pack up all their gear, and board "cattle cars" (large troop-carrying trucks that carried forty-four to fifty men) and journey north. If we were lucky we got to ride in a bus instead of the cattle cars. Recruits took all their possessions in their sea bags. Our gear was packed by the House Mice and King Rat, and put into the trucks that carried the gear.

The basis of being a Marine was being a rifleman. Every single Marine, no matter what their rank, or profession in the Marine Corps, was proficient with a rifle. That was one of the things that really set the Marine Corps apart from the other services. The recruits were going to go through some very intense lessons in how to shoot the rifle accurately. They had to pass a minimum qualification with the rifle in order to proceed in training. That was a phase that recruits looked forward to. It was a time of transition from the first phase, which was the most intense time for the recruits, into a phase with a more relaxed atmosphere. They were now capable of marching adequately, they knew protocol very well, and were shaping up rapidly. The recruits were also given a uniform perk: they were allowed to blouse their trousers around their boots. That meant that they put an elastic cord around their boots and then tucked their trouser leg under the cord. This gave them a look that more closely resembled real Marines. It changed their appearance from the sloppy look of "First Phase" to the status of "Second Phase".

When I was a recruit in 1968, there were so many recruits going through training that there was not sufficient space to house them in the barracks at the rifle range, so an area was set up west of the barracks for tents—this was known as "Tent City". The tents were not very good living conditions: they were next to the freeway, and just off the Pacific Ocean. Ocean breezes made them very uncomfortable to live in, and the freeway sounds were constant during the night and day. I was very fortunate that my boot camp series was able to be housed in a barracks. Those were a big upgrade from our Quonset huts at MCRD.

At that time in the Marine Corps recruits also had to do one weeks service of either Mess Duty, or Maintenance Duty. Those that got Maintenance Duty were put to work making targets, or doing maintenance work. Their jobs were fairly easy in that they worked pretty normal hours. The rest were put on Mess Duty and had to work in the mess hall. That duty was very hard as the hours were extremely long, and recruits generally were standing on their feet all day long and well in to the night. The days started around 0330 (3:30 AM) and ended around 2130 (9:30 PM), or even later. That duty involved serving meals, swabbing the mess hall decks, cleaning pots and pans, peeling potatoes, and just about anything they could think of that was mess hall related. Most recruits absolutely hated the job.

During Mess and Maintenance week we drill instructors got a break. Since there was no training that week, only supervising at night, we usually got to take off for two to three days that week. Sometimes the platoon commander wanted to spend that time at the range and he would give the junior drill instructors the week off.

Once the Mess and Maintenance week was out of the way, it was time to get down to the matter of teaching the recruits how to shoot their weapons. Special instructors called Primary Marksman Instructors (PMI's) were in charge of the marksmanship training. The first week of the two week training course was going to be "snapping-in week". That was when the recruits learned how the weapon must be held to shoot it properly, how to aim the rifle correctly, and how to squeeze the trigger. They actually practiced shooting with empty rifles. They would aim at miniature targets that were in the middle of a large circle in which the recruits would surround in a large "snapping-in circle". There were three basic shooting positions that were taught: standing, prone (lying down on the belly) and sitting. Their slings were adjusted to keep the rifle taught so there was little movement of the rifle to send the bullets off their course. Much time was spent just practicing squeezing the triggers (as opposed to "snapping" the triggers which would cause the rifle to move, and the bullet to veer off the course desired). Recruits were taught how the sights worked on their rifles, and how the sights were going to be adjusted for the different distances they would be shooting the following week. By the end of the first week of snapping-in they were very accustomed to how their rifle was going to operate.

With the snapping-in week completed, the real task of shooting was in order. The second week would be shooting the rifles, and going through the actual qualification process. The first four days were not going to count. The real rifle qualification was on Friday. Many recruits had never fired a rifle before, and they had various reactions to the kick from the high powered rifles they were shooting. They had to practice shooting of the weapon to get accustomed to the recoil of the rifle when it was fired.

The first round of shooting took place at the 200 yard line. The targets were 200 yards from the point where the recruits were shooting from. They would fire their weapons from both the standing position, and the sitting positions. Standing position would be slow firing which meant they had plenty of time to shoot their allotted 10 rounds accurately at their targets. There was no rush to get the rounds off. Next they went to the sitting position, and that would be at rapid fire. That meant they had one minute to shoot 10 rounds of ammunition at the target.

The third round was at the 300 yard mark. That consisted of two positions: slow-fire prone, with the recruits lying on their bellies, and rapid-fire, sitting, which required them to shoot 10 rounds in one minute. Procedurally it was like it was at the 200 yard line.

Last up was the 500 yard line. That was slow fire in the prone position. At 500 yards it was difficult for the recruit to see the targets, let alone clearly identifying their own target. There were roughly fifty targets in a row across the range. They were identified by a number board that alternated black and white so as to give a contrast at the longer distances. It was not uncommon for a recruit to shoot at the wrong target at the 500 yard line.

As the distances got longer the bullet had a greater drop in trajectory. At a distance of 500 yards the bullet was going to drop about 2 feet, or more, on its way to the target. So the recruits were learning exactly how much adjustment they had to make in the elevation settings on their rifle sights. There was a knob on the sight that, when turned, equaled certain rise, or fall in the pointing of the barrels which affected the trajectory up, and down. In addition, there was an influence of the wind on the side movements of the bullets. On a windy day the sights had to be adjusted to compensate for that wind influence or the bullets would miss their marks. There were shooting coaches that were assigned to the recruits, and they stood, or knelt right next to them the whole time they were shooting. The coaches made sure that the recruits were adjusting their sights correctly, holding the weapons properly, and squeezing their triggers. They were also there as a safety precaution to make sure the recruits didn't fire in the *wrong* direction.

Each round the recruit fired was plotted by the recruit in a special book he kept at his side. He identified where he was aiming, and when the target came up with a patch showing where the bullet hit, he marked his plot showing where the bullet actually hit. If he was consistently aiming at the center, and the rounds were hitting at 3:00 position he needed to adjust the sights to bring the rounds into the center. His coaches were keeping an eye on this for him as well. By the time Friday came he would have his sights properly sighted in, and should be able to get a qualifying score. The coaches were also the ones that issued the ammo—they kept exact track of how much ammo each person was issued, and how many rounds were shot. They had to ensure that no unfired rounds left the area.

The range was not all shooting. There were a couple of important jobs that were taking place, and everyone was involved in these processes. First off, each time a round was fired the empty shell was ejected out of the rifle, and landed on the ground. After each shooting phase was complete at a yardage line, all the recruits had to pick up the casings, and put them into a barrel. Everything was recycled in the Marine Corps. Also, the targets didn't run themselves: they had to be manually operated. So the platoons were divided into two groups: the first group shot, and the second group manned the targets.

The targets were located at the end of the shooting range, and were known as the butts. To get to the butts everyone had to travel through a long tunnel that went between the various firing ranges that were along side of them. The tunnel was long, and had few lights to see by. Each butt (target) was manned by a recruit. The butts were large—about six feet wide by six feet tall. They were made of paper laid over a wooden frame, and nailed or glued onto the frame to give them a sturdy support. These targets were made by recruits on maintenance duty. The targets sat on a mechanism called a "butt" that allowed them to be raised and lowered by a recruit, with some ease of operation. Each time the bullet struck the target (on slow fire shooting) the recruits pulled the butts down, marked the place where the round hit the target, then raised the target, and placed a large black or white circular object over that spot. The shooter then knew exactly where his round hit, and made adjustments to his sights if they were missing the point he was aiming at. If the shooter missed the target altogether then he got a "Maggie's Drawers". That was a red flag that was waived left to right over the face of the target. That was the worst thing that could happen to a shooter, and was embarrassing when it occurred. Working in the butts was not the safest job in the world either. A NATO round as fired in the M-14 rifle travels at 2800 feet per second when it leaves the barrel, and is still traveling over a quarter of a mile per second when it hits the target. If the bullet hits the 2 X 4 boards that made up the edges of the butt it could splinter the wood, causing the bullet to fly into the butts. Or the bullet would go straight through the target as normal, and hit the embankment behind the butts, which was there to catch all the lead going through the air. However, after years of bullets hitting the banks, there was a lot of lead there. It became encrusted with lead, and often could cause a bullet to ricochet back into the butts. When I was a drill instructor walking the butts in a supervising capacity, I was hit numerous times by flying bullets that had either ricocheted off the target edge, or bounced back from the banks. I considered it very dangerous in that job, and never liked being in the butts outside of the area the recruits were in. The recruits were under a ledge, and were pretty well protected against the forward movements of the bullet trajectories.

One of the fears of all of us was the fear that a recruit could try and retaliate for some perceived injustice in training by his drill instructor. That point was made in the movie "Full Metal Jacket", where the drill instructor was shot to death by a recruit on graduation day. As a result of that fear, we stood well back from the shooting lines on the ranges. The coaches were there to ensure our safety as well. At the end of the day, all the recruits were given a complete shake-down before they could leave the range. They had to remove their boots, empty their pockets and turn them inside out, and then they were frisked. I am completely satisfied that it was almost impossible for a recruit to bring a live round back to the area. There was just too much supervision on the lines, and the rounds were very carefully counted out at the point of issue. The coaches monitored each shot the recruit made, so there was not much chance of this happening. *We still stood way back.*

The shooting range was run by a Range Officer who was in charge. There was also a Safety Officer whose job it was to ensure that every safety precaution was being taken to preserve everyone's safety. My confidence in their ability was shaken one day however. One of the range personnel had brought his personal weapon to the range—a really nice high powered hunting rifle with a scope mounted on the top of it. The Safety Officer was conversing with the coach, and talked the coach into letting him shoot a couple of rounds to try it out. When the firing line was given the okay to begin shooting, the officer took close aim, and squeezed off a round. Suddenly we saw him roll over on his side, and grab for his face, and he was in obvious pain. When he stood up he had a huge circular gash around his entire eye socket, and blood was pouring out. What he had done was put his eye up to the rifle scope, resting his eye against the metal surface (instead of staying back the required 3–4 inches from the end of the scope). He was obviously not familiar with high powered hunting rifles with scopes. When he squeezed the trigger on the high powered rifle, the recoil of the weapon forced the edges of the telescopic sight into his face, and lacerated his face with a perfect circle about ½ inch deep. He had to be sent to the corpsman immediately because the cut required sutures. So much for Safety Officers!

I did have one incident with a recruit. He was just about to shoot from the prone position at the 300 yard line. In that position the shooter had the sling of the rifle firmly strapped to his arm so that he could apply pressure against the sling while it was tight, and he could get a steady tripod-like hold on the rifle. The sling was short, and there was little play. When he dropped down into position his rifle muzzle hit the ground, and some debris got inside the muzzle. He reached forward with his arm that had the sling strapped to it, and was struggling to reach the muzzle to clear the debris. He pulled harder and harder on his left arm, straining to reach the muzzle. Unfortunately for him, he forgot to remove his finger from the trigger on his right hand. At the extreme strain needed to reach the muzzle with his left hand, his right hand *squeezed* the trigger. The result was a perfect 7.62 mm hole blasted into his index finger. *Ouch!* He was out of action for several months waiting for his finger to heal. There were no purple hearts for shooting yourself at a rifle range.

One general change in the stress of recruit training took place the closer we got to qualification day—our thinking was that we wanted the recruits to be loose. If they were too stressed out then they would not shoot well. It was important that all the recruits shot well. Platoon pride was on the line. The platoon was up against three other platoons, and they were all vying to "take the range" and win the pennant for being the best shooting platoon in the series. Since being a riflemen was what being a Marine was all about, that was going to be a big event. Everyone was psyched up for that. The night before qualifications there was no PT, no Pit, nothing. We sat the recruits down, and just talked to them. We wanted them relaxed. We talked about how important qualifying was for each person individually, and for the platoon as a whole. They were well aware that anyone that did not qualify was going to be set back in training until they did qualify. Big things were on the line here. Plus, they also knew that we were turning the corner on the training, and were just about to the third phase, and that meant they were getting close to ending it all, and graduating. Things were looking up, at least for today.

Qualification day came like any other day. Reveille was at 0400 (4:00 AM). We got up, and went to the mess hall early. The barracks were quickly cleaned and readied for the day. We marched to the shooting range which was across the roadway. No matter what the weather, qualifying day *was* the day.

The first group set up at the 200 yard line, and the other half double-timed to the butts. Everyone was waiting for the starting signal: "Ready on the right. Ready on the left. Ready on the firing line. Shooters may begin to shoot when your targets appear." Suddenly it sounded like a war zone. Tensions were high. We sat and watched. That was going to be a long day. The shooting process went to the different yard lines, and continued. At the end of the 500 yard shooting we knew who had qualified in the first group. Then we repeated the process for the second group. By 1400 (2:00 PM) qualifying was all over. We knew where we stood as a platoon. We knew who did, and who did not qualify. We went back to the barracks, and got ready to move out the next morning for our return to MCRD, San Diego.

That night we handed out praise to the top shooters. Qualifiers were going to get to call home the next day when we got back to San Diego. Non-qualifiers were re-introduced to the Pit. Things were going to get back to normal now. Things were going to tighten up. *The party was over.*

PHASE THREE:
THE END WAS NEAR

The third phase of recruit training began when the recruits returned from the rifle range. That was a much awaited phase for the recruits because they knew the end was near, and graduation was now within sight. They also were allowed to unbutton the top button of their utility blouse, and they were taking on the look of *real* Marines.

During the final phase recruits would be issued their full issue of uniforms. They would also get final instructions in various subjects. In addition, they would be tested on their knowledge learned during training. They would also be tested for their physical fitness and would go through the final drill evaluation.

The rifle range was a phase in which the recruits were given a little more slack than normal during the week they were firing the rifles and going through qualification. That was necessary so that they could relax enough to shoot well and qualify with their weapons. The recruits had somewhat grown accustomed to the more relaxed atmosphere: but it was still Marine Corps boot camp, and there were still about three more weeks to go. A lot had to be accomplished in the remaining short time left. We were going to bear down hard—*very hard*. Suddenly, nothing they did was good enough for us and they got a new taste of the Pit. Marine Corps boot camp discipline was back.

The clothing issue in third phase was to give the recruits their full array of uniforms they would need for the duration of their initial enlistments. To that point they had only been issued their utility uniforms for the daily workload. Other military branches provide the full set early in their training cycles, but the Marines knew that the recruit bodies were going to change during the course of training, and the uniforms would not likely fit properly after training was done. The dress uniform had to be tailored to fit correctly, and that was a time consuming ordeal. The Marine Corps takes pride in their uniform, *way* more than any other service. Sloppy fitting uniforms were not acceptable, and the tailoring had to be exact. In addition, the recruits were going to be facing a final inspection in which the uniforms would be inspected for proper fit. Dress shoes would also be issued. When the recruits initially received their shoes, the shoes had a regular leather patina like any black shoe in a shoe store. They would be taught how to spit-shine their shoes to a high gloss.

Once the tailoring was completed the recruits had to go back and have the fit double-checked. Everything had to be right before they proceeded. If everything fit the clothing was brought back to the Quonset huts and readied for stamping their names in the proper locations. Each recruit had been issued a name-stamp kit during First Phase. They had to carefully stamp their names on the uniforms. The names had to be perfectly stamped in order to pass the next inspection. Inevitably, there would always be a recruit that stamped his name upside down, or put it on the wrong side of the clothing item. These were maddening moments for us, as the ink was indelible, and there was little recourse except to have the recruit purchase another item of clothing so it would be right.

One of the final inspections that recruits had to go through during the Vietnam era was called a "Junk-on-the-Bunk" inspection. That required that the recruits lay out all of their uniforms: covers, shoes, boots, belts and other issued items, onto their bunks. The arrangement was a very precise array. Everything had to be folded and creased perfectly, and in a very specific order. Hours were spent on inspection preparation. We drill instructors were relentless in getting the recruits to get it right—we were all over them for the slightest error or discrepancy. It took days of preparation for that, and each day the layout had to be placed back on the bunk. The night before the inspection most recruits did not sleep on their bunks so that the array could be kept perfectly. We would go from Quonset hut to Quonset hut, pre-inspecting the bunk layouts. Woe to the recruit that had anything out-of-order or placed incorrectly.

As soon as the junk-on-the-bunk inspection was completed, one set of uniforms had to be sent to the cleaners so that the recruits had a uniform to wear for the Final Inspection that would be held shortly after. Recruits would spend hours of their free-time spit-shining their shoes. They also had to spit-shine the visors of their garrison covers which were the covers worn with the dress uniform. Spit-shining was somewhat of an art. It required a certain light touch, and proper motions to get it right. The cloth used had to be damp: not too damp, and not too dry. That was where we showed our prowess: teaching that required patience, and yet still had to be done with the proper discipline to get it right.

Final Inspection was a serious inspection. It was done by the Battalion Commander and Battalion Sergeant Major. They would be accompanied by the Platoon Commander, inspecting one recruit at a time down each squad. The Battalion Commander would ask questions about Marine Corps history and their general orders. The recruit had to answer correctly: failure to do so would result in a poor ranking for the platoon as a whole against the results of our series. More importantly, a poor showing here would result in a visit to the Pit later. Unlike the first inspection in Phase One when the purpose was to tear down the recruits to show them what they needed to work on, the Final Inspection was designed to show the recruits what a typical inspection in the Marine Corps would be like. Inspections were something they were going to encounter many times in their Marine careers. They would soon find out that passing an inspection would be necessary, in many cases, to be issued a liberty card which would entitle the Marine to go off base on liberty. Inspections were an everyday aspect in the normal life of the Marines.

The Practical Exam was another form of testing the recruits' knowledge of practical matters such as how to apply a field dressing on a wound; how to pick up and carry a wounded Marine; how to fold a backpack, etc. Many hours would be spent by us to ready the platoon for that test. A recruit had to pass in order to graduate: a failure could result in being set back in training. That also tested the skills of the DI's since we were the ones that taught the recruits those skills. Any failure on the recruit's part was a failure on our part. We approached that with an attitude of "failure was not an option".

Another final test the recruits had was the Physical Fitness Test (PFT). That was the same test they had when they first arrived, but the expectation was now greater. They now had to run a three mile run in under twenty-seven minutes— most would run it in about twenty minutes. Any failure here was an automatic set-back in training. The recruits were always ready for that one! They had spent the previous three months doing more exercises than they had done in their whole lifetime, making it was almost inconceivable that they would not pass that test. The PFT was also a test in which the platoon was judged as a whole against the other platoons in the series and it was something they wanted to excel at.

Final Drill was one of the most important tests the recruits would face. That was a pride test in which the discipline and skill of the platoon as a whole would be judged against the rest of their series. Close order drill was one of the mainstays of the Marine Corps training, and it represented the epitome of discipline and following orders. Taking the honor of being the best marching platoon in the series was a major victory for both the platoon and our status as the drill instructors.

Third Phase also had one major perk for some lucky recruits: visitor's day. That occurred on a Sunday just before the end of training when visitors could come to the base and visit their Marine recruit. Unlike the other services, the Marine Corps did not allow visitors at any other time in training. Recruits have not had any contact with family or friends other than through the mail or, if the recruit was lucky and qualified at the rifle range, he might have gotten to make a 10 minute phone call home. Normally the only recruits that had visitors were those that lived within a reasonable distance from MCRD, San Diego. I was fortunate when I was a recruit in that I lived in San Diego, so when my visitor day came I was able to see my new bride. That was the best possible day I had in boot camp, as I remember. Nothing can describe the elation of seeing loved ones after all that we had been through. The visitation was only a few hours long, and recruits were confined to a patio-like area not far from our Quonset huts.

Graduation ceremonies were conducted during that era in the Depot Theater which was located at the south end of the parade deck. The recruits were marched into the theater and seated by platoon. All of us drill instructors were seated on the stage with the Platoon Commanders. Those recruits that had done exceptionally well at the rifle range, physical fitness testing, etc, were given special plaques for their outstanding performances. The drill instructors and Platoon Commanders were introduced, along with the Series Officer and the Series Gunnery Sergeant. In the rear of the auditorium were family members and friends that managed to make it, never more than about 150 to 200 visitors. Once the inside ceremonies were completed, the recruits were filed outside into platoon formations, marched around to the front of the theater, and placed in series formation. The platoons' Gideon was presented back to a drill instructor of each platoon and we marched off to retire the Gideon's. One by one the Platoon Commanders dismissed their platoons, and in a roar of delight, the recruits had taken on the status of "Marine" for the first time. They were entitled to go on base-liberty which confined them to staying on the base. That was the first freedom these men had had in over three months.

Later in the evening, after base liberty was over, the platoons were gathered around the Platoon Commander. He would give the Marines their military occupational specialties (MOS), and told them where their orders were sending each one of them. Most were going to go to Vietnam after their training for their MOS was completed. For most of them, combat would be a part of their lives within two to three more months. Unfortunately, some would never return from that first duty assignment.

The day after graduating the recruits said goodbye to us, then boarded buses to be transported to Camp Pendleton for their infantry training. They had made it through their toughest gauntlet in Marine Corps training. For us drill instructors it was a sad day: we would now have to pick up a brand new platoon, starting the process all over again.

ENDLESS DUTY

The life of a drill instructor was harsh to say the least. There were generally three of us assigned to each platoon of eighty-five to ninety men. The senior man was the Platoon Commander. He was usually a staff sergeant or sometimes a gunnery sergeant. The two junior men were assigned as junior drill instructors, and due to my being junior to just about everybody, I was always a junior drill instructor. The Platoon Commander was identified by his wearing a black duty belt, highly spit-shined to a high gloss. The drill instructors wore a standard ammo belt as their duty belt. The belts were worn every minute the drill instructors were on duty. When wearing the duty belts the DI's were entitled to remain covered (hats stay on) indoors. The duty belt had to contain a "field dressing" bandage in an attachment to the belt. The field dressing was often replaced by a pack of cigarettes, which were about the same size as the field dressing.

Junior drill instructors were typically the "heavies" who carried out the real harassment parts, letting the Platoon Commander stay in the background as much as possible. Not that the Platoon Commander did not get in their faces, it was just that the junior drill instructors were more likely to carry that out. All the drill instructors performed the same basic job of training recruits.

Duty was broken down into three cycles: twenty-four hours on; twenty-four hours standby; and twenty-four hours off. That meant that on our day of duty we started at 0700 (7:00 AM), and remained the man in charge of getting the platoon to all the training classes, and other places that they were needed to be taken to during the next twenty-four hours. We spent the night with the platoon when we were on duty. That stay with the platoon would not end until the next night around 1900 hours (7:00 PM) when we were in the second cycle on "standby". In that cycle, the drill instructor that had been on duty the previous twenty-four hours, was there as a standby, to back up the current duty DI. Many of the activities called for a minimum of two drill instructors per platoon, and standby duty was the second man. The off day was the favorite—being off for a whole day. Getting some rest. Resting the voice. Relaxing. There was a catch though—we were not always allowed to be off. Sometimes, no matter what the duty cycle we were in, all three DI's would be needed for training.

There was a tremendous physical toll on us drill instructors. In the first phase we were using our voices so much that we would become very hoarse—so hoarse that we lost our voices to a major degree. That could be very problematic as the voice was the biggest weapon we had to keep recruits on their toes. It was always easy to determine what phase we were in with our platoon by the sound of our voice. The strain was actually so harsh on the vocal cords that it took me over two years, from the time I left the Marine Corps, before my voice came back to even what might be remotely considered normal.

We had to do our job, no matter what our physical condition was. We were leaders, and could not ever fail to keep up the pace. No matter how sick we felt, we were there. One of the hazards we faced was the infusion of new germs each time a new platoon was picked up. Recruits came from everywhere (west of the Mississippi in the case of San Diego MCRD recruits), and they brought with them new strains of germs. Shortly after each platoon was picked up, we fell victim to those germs. It seemed like I caught more colds and flu bugs during this tour of duty, than at any other time in my life. We had to set the tone however, and we kept going no matter how bad we felt.

One of the things that seemed to always happen on our off-day was being needed by the Company, Battalion, or Regiment for some special needs. There was always a person needed to attend a training class, or some special drill that was taking place. Sometimes these special assignments went to the "junior" man. I was *always* the junior man. I had less time in the Marines than anybody else on the field, and that made me vulnerable to these assignments. Being the junior man also seemed to affect the changing of schedules, so that all the holidays fell to me. I cannot remember having one single holiday at home—not a Christmas, New Years, Thanksgiving, etc. I stood duty on all of them. I did not spend a Christmas day at home until after I left the Marine Corps. But there were perks to being on duty on the holidays: there was no training schedule, and the mess hall always prepared a special meal. Steak was usually offered, and it was done up very nice. So, at least I can say I ate very well on those special occasions.

During the period of the Vietnam War, there were constant war protests taking place at colleges, and universities throughout America. That also was the case at local campuses in San Diego. One of the extra little duties that were put upon us drill instructors was being assigned to the "Riot Control Squad". Riot control was banded together to be used in case of a riot, most likely at a local college, or university. The protests throughout the nation had become very ugly at times, and had even resulted in students being shot to death at Kent State University. The war in Vietnam was still in full swing in the early 1970's, and there were reports that some of the local schools were going to have protest rallies. Local officials requested the assistance of the Marine Corps, and the resulting riot control training was ordered. I am not sure why we drill instructors were needed for this duty, but there we were, ready for action. I found the training to be very interesting, as they taught us how to approach a rioting crowd, slowly "stomp-marching" forward. Stomp-marching was a technique of stomping the feet down creating a loud thud, which was magnified by the many members of the riot squad line marching in unison. It was ominous sounding. We each had a plastic face shield attached to a full metal helmet, and a large wooden baton. Stomp-marching was done very slowly, pushing the baton forward with each step with the left foot. The sound of the stomping, coupled with the slow onerous movements of the squad, could easily put fear into a rioting mass. The idea was to slowly move the masses backward, and outward, thus dispersing the group. We practiced the movements over and over. For over four days during this period we were required to stay on stand-by status, never leaving the barracks we were assigned to for more than ten minutes. In the end, there were no riots, and we were not needed for deployment. I could not help but think of the irony of the fact that I was assigned to combat the protesters, and yet I really felt I was one of the protesters of the war in my heart.

Duty as a DI can seem endless. We were always there. There was never enough time to do all we needed to do. It could actually get worse than it normally was—there were times of "overlap". Overlap was when we were still in the Final Phase of training with one platoon, and then got assigned to pick up a new platoon a week or more before the first platoon graduated. Those were the toughest times of all. One day we would be on duty with a third-phase platoon that was very well organized, looked sharp performing, could march perfectly, and responded immediately to orders; then, the next day we were on duty with a new herd that didn't know up from down. The swing was almost too much to bear. There was no time off: no seeing our wives—nothing. We were on duty twenty-four hours a day, seven days a week. The Vietnam War was in full swing during those times and recruits were coming in by the droves. Billeting all the recruits was also very problematic. New barracks were being built, but were not completed yet, and recruits were living in every Quonset hut available at MCRD.

Somehow we seemed to love and thrive in the pressure. We bitched about it amongst ourselves, but it was thrilling to be so involved in something so important. At the time however, I did not fully comprehend the significance of the job I was doing. That realization would take a number of years to fully take place. Most of us just thought of ourselves as just doing our jobs.

Some of the drill instructors did not fair so well in the pressures of the drill field. One such drill instructor was named Sergeant Billy Bobo. Sgt Bobo had returned from Vietnam service, and was thrown into Drill Instructor School somewhat against his desires. He was a highly decorated Marine, and had done heroic things in Vietnam. But, he also suffered deeply from his experiences in Vietnam, and was very much affected by them. As a drill instructor he was very sadistic in handling his recruits, and often seemed to go over the edge of common sense in some of the things that he would do. He knew his stuff, but seemed to not be able to control his actions well. He could be scary at times. Sergeant Bobo lived twenty miles from the base, and rode a Harley Davidson motorcycle to work. He was having marital problems as well. He often spoke of his wife, and would say how he wanted to "blow her head off". But, we all just shrugged it off, as Sgt Bobo just bitching about his troubles. Sergeant Bobo was interested in guns too. He bought a .357 magnum revolver. That was nothing unusual, in that as most Marines were also into weapons, and most had their own arsenals. One day he came to me, and made a proposal: he was commuting on his motorcycle during a very bad weather cycle in San Diego in which our rainfall was three times the normal. He was riding his Harley Davidson motorcycle to work every day, and the rain was killing him. I had a 1965 Falcon Ranchero that was mostly a hot-rod with a souped up motor. My car got about 6 miles per gallon, and I was thinking of selling it. He proposed a trade with me. I jumped at the chance, as the motorcycle was worth way more than my Ranchero, and I stood to make a profit as soon as I could sell the bike. So we swapped vehicles, and signed over the pink slips. He delivered the bike to my house that night, as I did not know how to ride a motorcycle. He was still complaining of his marital problems, and kept referring to his wife as "the bitch". I, like everyone else, did not think too much of it—after all, some people just complain about everything. I felt sorry for him because I knew he was suffering inside from his Vietnam experiences.

Two days after I made the vehicle trade I was standing duty. At 0400 (4:00 AM) the Duty NCO came in the Duty Hut to wake us up. I will never forget what he said as we jumped out of our racks: "Sergeant Bobo is in jail. He pistol-whipped his wife and literally blew her head off her body, doing it in front of his two kids!" We never saw nor heard from Sergeant Bobo again. That left a lasting impression on me because I knew that deep down, that Sgt Bobo was a *victim* of the war. It reconfirmed in my mind why I was so opposed to the war—even the Marines that came back alive, and unmaimed, were affected by it. Unfortunately, innocent people were affected by it too. I have often wondered what happened to his children after witnessing such a horrific thing.

There was always someone on duty in the Marine Corps. Every unit everywhere has someone on watch at all times. In the case of recruits, they had what was known as the "fire watch". That function was shared by all the recruits on a rotating basis. They each had fire watch for one hour during the hours from taps to reveille. The purpose was to have someone always awake in case of a fire. But, they also act somewhat like a guard. At the end of their watch they woke up the next fire watch recruit, and so on, through the night. One of the functions of the last man on fire watch was to go to the Duty Hut and wake up the drill instructors at 0400 (4:00 AM).

There were some drill instructors that had serious mental issues, and could not be woken up by shaking them. Those DI's had been seriously affected in Vietnam by what they had experienced. If they were touched to be awakened they would jump up as if they were being attacked, and reach out to *kill* the attacker. That was a very scary occurrence when it happened. Those drill instructors had to be awakened by making noise at a distance, for safety sake. Some of those Marines were actually *very scary*. It made me very nervous to stay the night in the Duty Hut with them.

Once reveille was held for us, we were up and about and getting ready for the day ahead. I always prepared my uniforms the night before, so all I had to do was take a shower, shave, and get dressed. I always anxiously awaited the reveille call that came over the PA system at 0500 (5:00 AM). The minute it sounded, all four drill instructors in the Duty Hut would stand at the hatches, and yell "Lights on, hatches open." That command was repeated by the recruits in each Quonset hut all the way down the row. What a way to start the day, I always thought. We would then immediately start jumping into their Quonset huts to ensure that everyone was up and moving. Woe was the private who tried to get a few more minutes of sleep before jumping out of the rack! We made sure that from the opening bell, we were *visible* and especially *audible*. There was never a doubt we were everywhere all at once. Nothing got by us. Noise was our ally, and we made lots of it. Nothing on the planet compares to being roused by a Marine Corps drill instructor.

WEARING THE SMOKEY

When one thinks of a drill instructor, the image that comes across is always of a Marine with a campaign hat, known by most people as a "Smokey the Bear" hat. That cover was initiated for use by DI's in the late 1950's, and was immortalized by the movie "The DI" starring Jack Webb. It has become the symbol of the Marine drill instructors and was the pride of every Marine drill instructor who wore one.

The campaign cover was issued upon graduation from the Drill Instructor School. Most drill instructors also bought a second, or even a third hat, to always have a cover that was clean, and in top shape. It took a lot of hard work to keep the cover looking as it was designed: with the brim flat at all times. The hats were made out of wool and were of high quality. But, the brims would tend to bend upward with exposure to moisture such as normal humidity, and certainly with rain. Properly worn, the brim was absolutely flat, and the cover was worn squarely on the head with the brim supposed to be parallel to the deck. Most DI's put a slightly forward cant to them, giving a more "meaningful" appearance.

To recruits in boot camp, any person wearing a Smokey was a person of authority. There was no need to try to determine what that person did because, if you were at a recruit depot, then that person was a drill instructor.

The campaign cover was a magical cover. It took on a special meaning while being worn. It was symbolic of power, authority and the Marine drill instructor was defined by it.

Taking care of a campaign cover required some extra work by us. It required brushing to remove the heavy amounts of dust, and dirt that fell onto it with the activities surrounding recruit training. Most of us also had a special device they used that clamped down on the brim, to flatten any tendency it had of bending upwards. One trick that was used was to spray hair spray on the underside of the brim: for some reason hair spray would hold the brim flat.

The recruits had taps at 2100 (9:00) each night. Once the lights went out, they hit the racks, and slept until reveille the next morning. But, we still had much to

122

do after taps. Uniforms needed to be ironed, and shoes and boots were in need of spit-shining.

Drill instructors received free laundry services and shoe repair as part of their job perks. That was due to the heavy use of uniforms and shoes while we trained recruits. I had to have my shoes resoled about every sixty days, as they wore out from all the marching and walking around that we did. The same with the boots, but they usually lasted about ninety days. I never wore a uniform more than once before I took it in for cleaning. I had about a dozen uniforms of each type, and they were always at-the-ready for wearing.

Upon getting a uniform back from the laundry I would take it back to the Duty Hut and hang it in the locker, waiting for later to press it out after taps. All of us had an iron in our lockers, and there was always an ironing board handy. If we didn't have an ironing board, we used our foot lockers and put a towel on the wooden surface. All the creases in the blouses and trousers were re-ironed to make them straight, and perfect. The cleaners did a reasonable job of pressing, but they usually left small wrinkles in the clothing, and the result was nowhere near the standard of quality a good drill instructor wanted to have. Every square inch of the uniform was re-pressed again. The utility uniform came back from the cleaners with an extremely heavy starching which caused the material to feel stiff, and board-like. From my days in the Drill Instructor School, I was ingrained with the belief that a drill instructor must look perfect at all times. Even though the utility uniform was the working uniform for heavy activities, I still wanted to look my best while wearing it. I had a spray bottle of a concoction of water and starch, and would spray the uniform and press it again, resulting in sheen on the uniform that made it really stand out.

After pressing the uniforms, I had to take care of the shoes and boots. Spit-shining the leather was the only acceptable way to make the shoes and boots look good. Spit-shining took a while to get the hang of doing it right. Too much rubbing and the wax could come off, pitting the surface. I got it down to where I could spit-shine my boots, or shoes, in about 10 minutes each. They had a perfect shine to them, and looked like patent leather. I maintained three pairs of shoes and three pairs of boots at all times.

It was important to always look good. Once we put the uniform on, we did not sit down, so that the trousers would not get "sit-down creases" on them. When we returned from any activity, we often had sweat marks on the uniforms, or our shoes, or boots would be dusty. We changed uniforms a lot. Recruits never really understood that, as they were always in awe of our spic-and-span appearances all the time. It required a lot of work to accomplish: it took staying up till midnight each night to get the job done right.

Reveille for us was at 0400 (4:00 AM), which was one hour before the recruits were woken. The difference in the reveille times was so the we could be totally ready for the day, so the minute reveille sounded over the PA system; we were out on the roadways bellowing "Lights on, hatches open, rise and shine!"

My first realization as to the power of the "hat" came one day in 1971 as I was marching my platoon to the new mess hall. The depot had built new barracks for recruit training, to replace the Quonset huts we had been living in. But, before the recruits were allowed to use the new barracks, the barracks were initially used to house returning Vietnam veterans. Marines that were waiting discharge after serving out their tours of duty. Drill instructors hated that arrangement because those Marines were known as "short timers", which meant that they were getting out very soon, and had attitudes that reflected that. They did not care about anything other than getting out, and going home. With our charge to motivate recruits, and make them believe that the Marine Corps was always going to be full of strict standards they would have to live by, it was disheartening to see these young Marines sitting outside the barracks with their uniforms a mess, or often out-of-uniform altogether. On one occasion, there were three lance corporals milling around by the side of the roadway that platoons used to get to the mess hall. They were somewhat mocking the recruits as we marched by on our way to the mess hall. I could not help myself: I stopped my platoon, and walked straight up to the lance corporals, and asked in my best DI command voice: *Why are you Marines outside without your covers on?*" They immediately snapped their heels together, and stood at the position of attention, and replied "Sir, sorry, sir. We did not think it was necessary since we are getting out soon. We will get them right away, sir." I was very surprised. Here were three men that had just come back from combat. They had probably been sent to Vietnam straight out of training. They were used to the lax order of the combat zones and they had been through a lot. And yet, here they stood, standing there scared stiff when they were being addressed by a drill instructor: it was obviously still vivid in their minds what a DI was, and represented. They instinctively had reverted back to being *recruits* again while they were in the presence of a drill instructor. It was the campaign cover that made the difference. *The man with the Smokey!*

The significance of my job, and the impact it would have on those I led, was beginning to make its mark on me.

AFTER HOURS

When the job was finally done for the day some DI's headed to the NCO club. It was a place for camaraderie and relaxing. Most DI's could put away a lot of beer and the club was the place to do that. However, I was not a drinker and going home was my choice for relaxing.

Going home after thirty-six to forty-eight hours of drill instructor duty always created a major adjustment for every one of us. During our days we had one hundred percent obedience to our every order. Our recruits would respond instantaneously to us. We shouted our demands and we did not hesitate to point out deficiencies to our recruits. We were gods at work.

Once home we become "Honey". "Honey, take out the trash." "Honey, will you move the couch away from the wall?" "Honey, the light is out in the kitchen." All of a sudden, **we** became the House Mouse.

It was not easy to adjust to the difference in the response times we had grown accustomed to getting from our recruits and the times after we gave a "request" to our wives. They didn't care about the response times we got from our recruits— *our wives were not recruits!* As tough as the recruits may have seen us with our dazzling Marine DI persona, the same was not going to happen at home. A wife can be tougher than a DI when she wants to be, and any attempt to resort to Marine Corps recruit training tactics flew out the window at the home-front.

My wife Melody was like most of the DI's wives and she was fully aware of the stresses I was dealing with every day. She was very lenient on me during my "tone-down" period after getting home. She would listen to all my stories about the activities I went through, and yet still was able to get me to remember she was my wife and not my squad leader.

Since I did not hang out and drink with the guys at the NCO club after work it made it easier for me to adjust to the immediate home-front changes needed when I walked through the front door. It helped that I was also a home-town DI and all of my personal friends from high school and college were local. That allowed my wife and I to enjoy a more normal after-hours life than most DI's, most of whom came from someplace else. My wife and I had places we could go to that put me right back into my pre-Marine Corps mind-set. My friends were all civilians with no military experience and that allowed me to keep my frame of mind in check.

Most of my friends and the people I met found it hard to believe that I was actually a Marine drill instructor. I guess that most people thought a DI was a hard-ass *all the time*. It was difficult for them to envision that it was a persona that every drill instructor perfects and becomes when he puts the campaign cover on his head. It was hard for them to believe some of the stories I would tell about my daily experiences with the recruits. My civilian friends could not relate to the mentality of recruit training and how the recruits could tolerate our actions.

Many DI's had major adjustment problems when getting home. That was especially so if they stopped by the club and had a few too many beers. It is a well recognized fact now that the returning Vietnam veterans were often suffering from post-combat stress disorders. Couple that syndrome with the stresses and workload of a drill instructor and it became a monumental issue. Many DI's drank in excess to help themselves ease their problems. Drinking only made their problems much worse at home. It would create a vicious cycle—more stress, more drinking, then more stress from home. Their long hours away from home, and then their lack of adjustment when they got home, often resulted in very strained marriages. It was not uncommon for a DI's to report to work the next day very hung-over from their long night before. Worse yet, sometimes they did not even go home. Often, while we were located at the Edson Range, they just stayed in the duty office to avoid conflict at home.

Many of the Marines that were sent to Drill Instructor School with me had a fear that the job would be a major hindrance to their marriages due to the hours and stress they would have when they became DI's. Most were just returning directly from a tour of duty in Vietnam as well, and they just wanted to spend some quiet time with their wives and families. Some would make the adjustments and learn to live with the daily stresses, and then switch to the different role we had to play when we got home at night—but then, some could not. Those that could not make the adjustments ended up with a ruined marriage, a drinking problem or the added stresses sometimes provoked them to violate the SOP which often resulted in disciplinary action being imposed against them. A disciplinary action for violating the SOP could be as minor as being relieved from drill instructor duty to being court-martialed and stripped of rank, imprisonment, and possibly discharged from the Marine Corps. In many cases I believe that some of the DI's that got relieved from duty were realizing self-fulfilling prophesies.

I always felt that being in the Marine Corps was just like having a regular job—once the day was over you went home and became part of the family again. It was fairly easy to practice that philosophy, and it is something I still do to this day in every job. But, underneath all the adjustments that had to be made at home was still a Marine Corps drill instructor hell-bent on making the best recruits possible and eagerly awaiting reporting back to work to begin the experience all over again. *I could not wait to wake up and go back to work.*

"Honey, before you leave will you go pick up after the dog?"

THUMPING

The United States Marine Corps has always had a policy against abusing recruits. There have been several significant instances in Marine Corps history, in which the hazing of recruits by their drill instructors, have become notorious black eyes towards the methods used in training Marines. The most significant case was the McKeon case in 1956 at MCRD, Parris Island. Six recruits drowned in a night march conducted by their drill instructor, who was intoxicated at the time. As a means of instilling discipline, he had the platoon march into the marshes that surround Parris Island. The tide waters were moving, and the currents were strong. The platoon marched into a spot in which the bottom suddenly dropped off, and the water depth increased dramatically. Some of the recruits could not swim. In the confusion and chaos that ensued, six of the recruits drowned. That drew national attention to the methods used by the Marine Corps, and brought about the possibility that Congress might have legislated the Marine Corps out of existence.

The McKeon case confirmed the need to have a very standardized and monitored system for training recruits. The Standard Operating Procedure (SOP) was developed for recruit training. Drill Instructor School became the starting point of screening drill instructors to eliminate those with obvious tendencies toward potential maltreatment of recruits. Lesson plans were developed to teach the drill instructors acceptable methods of instruction, troop handling, and leadership. The Marine Corps was determined to clean up the bad public image that the McKeon case had brought them.

The SOP gave a set of rules to the drill instructors, on what was not acceptable handling of recruits. It gave limitations to the amount of physical training (PT) that could be administered for punishment, and discipline purposes. It prohibited hazing of recruits, and the co-mingling of recruit money with that of the drill instructors. The SOP covered just about every situation, and was a very clear order to follow. To enforce the SOP there were more officers assigned to recruit training to supervise the activities.

Training of Marine recruits has always been an "in your face" type of training that required the drill instructor to be loud, gruff, and aggressive. That did not change with the more intense scrutiny of the training. Drill instructors continued to act in the aggressive fashion that had made them the training icons they had always been made out to be.

The Vietnam War created a huge demand for manpower that required the Marine Corps to get recruits to the battle fields of Vietnam as quickly as possible. The result of this was that the recruit training syllabus was shortened to nine weeks, from the standard twelve weeks in normal times. By taking one-fourth of the training time away from the drill instructors created a huge problem: less time to train meant more had to be accomplished in a much shorter time. Discipline takes time to develop, and the training of recruits in the Marine Corps had always been centered on discipline. That resulted with an increase in techniques that brought about discipline in a much quicker time—a sort of "hands-on" approach.

Recruits came from many different backgrounds, but during the Vietnam era the public was so against the war effort that it was not considered patriotic to enlist in the armed forces, as it was construed to be aiding the war effort. The result of that was that the type of recruits that came in was either those that were going to be drafted in any event and wanted to choose their branch, or they were more often, young men that did not have other options in life. They were high school drop-outs for the most part as the average recruit was just 17 years of age and had only a tenth grade education level. These men had also been part of the youth movement of the Baby Boomer Generation, and they were used to resisting all types of authority. These young men were not like the young men that came in during World War II or the Korean War.

The "hands-on" approach was referred to as "thumping". Thumping was the act of handling a recruit by striking, slapping, choking, or any other means of physical contact. Some drill instructors used these techniques more so than others, but all drill instructors during that era used some form of thumping while training recruits. The movie "Full Metal Jacket" portrays a very realistic picture of thumping during the course of training—everything from the DI punching the recruit in the gut, to having the recruit "choke himself" in the hand of his DI.

Recruits would respond to thumping. It did not take a recruit long to get the picture, when he knew the drill instructor would come up to him, and be a little physical with him if he was screwing up. The TV series "Gomer Pyle" often portrayed the opposite—Private Pyle would often frustrate his drill instructor Gunnery Sergeant Carter and "Sergeant" Carter, as he was called by Pyle, would be frazzled and perplexed with what to do. That portrayal of a frazzled DI was outrageous—no drill instructor was frazzled by a recruit. Gomer Pyle would have had his *ass kicked*, in a heart-beat, if he acted like that in real boot camp.

Thumping had a wide range of techniques. One of the most common methods was for the drill instructor to take his pointer finger, and pound it repeatedly into the recruit chest as a means of making a point, while he was chewing out the recruit for his actions. Sometimes a DI would grab the recruit by his blouse with both hands, and shake him. There was also the practice of taking a finger, and pushing upwards under the recruit chin, while yelling corrections to him. There were some techniques used by some of the meaner-oriented DI's that were pretty gruesome: they would actually beat on the recruit by punching him repeated or striking him with a solid blow to the head or body. Most DI's did not use extremely gruesome thumping tactics, as there was a point where it actually could create the opposite result expected, and the recruit could always write home, complaining of the maltreatment. When the recruits would write home about being maltreated, their parents would write to the Commanding General, or to their Congressmen, and it would sometimes result in Congressional investigations. At any given time there were always investigations taking place regarding maltreatment.

Incentive training was often used as a means of instilling discipline. The SOP had strict allowances for the number of repetitions of a particular exercise that could be administered to recruits, based on their phase of training. That was pretty much ignored by most DI's, and the dosage of physical training to the recruits was most often far in excess of the SOP limits. There were many cases of drill instructors actually modifying the exercises to create additional pain. One example I have witnessed, both as a recruit, as it was administered to my own platoon, and also as a DI, was to order recruits to do push-ups by placing their bare knuckles on the asphalt decking. The weight of the recruit, and the motion of the exercise would result in cuts in the knuckles. That would often get exacerbated by the drill instructor kicking sand on the deck to add a little more grit to grind the knuckles. That was excruciating to the recruits, but it brought about unity very quickly. The result was always a more disciplined unit.

There were cases of recruits that came to the Duty Hut, and would just sort of "whimp-out" to the drill instructor. The DI would start yelling in the recruit's ear, and then other DI's in the office would surround the recruit, and start yelling in his other ear. The purpose of that was to let the recruit know he was not going to be let off, and that the power of the drill instructor was extreme. I have seen recruits over six feet tall, and looking like an NFL linebacker, actually break down, and cry like a baby under this duress. Extreme handling of recruits almost always brought about the desired affect: it let the recruit know, in no uncertain terms, that he was going to have to buckle down, and get his act together, or he was going to be in for a *very long* and *unpleasant time*. All the recruits found out very quickly that Marine Corps training was moving straight ahead at all times, and they were not going to slow that progress down.

Drill instructors that were caught maltreating recruits would be relieved of their duties, and would most often have to stand court-martial proceedings. If the accused drill instructor was found guilty of the charges, he could lose his rank, be discharged, and even sent to prison. It was something that all drill instructors kept in the back of their minds, at all times, when tempted to go over the top. The Series Officers, Company Commanders, and other officers from the Recruit Training Battalions, as well as the Recruit Training Regiment, were always on the look-out for signs of maltreatment.

If the drill instructors felt that Private Smith was going to file a complaint of maltreatment, they would often do counter-measures to minimize the problem. At an opportune moment, when the platoon was given incentive training for screwing up, the drill instructor would have the platoon stop the exercise just before the repetitions were completed, and state that Private Smith did not want to do the repetitions correctly. Private Smith would be ordered to come up and stand in front of the platoon, and he would be excused from the exercises. The platoon would be given the exercise again, this time doubling the amount of repetitions. Before beginning, the platoon would be ordered to thank Private Smith: "Thank you Private Smith" they would scowl, in a loud voice in unison, and they would then begin the exercising again. Over and over the process would be repeated at various times during the days. It did not take long at all for the recruits to absolutely hate Private Smith for his actions. When the time came for the investigation to begin, the Company Commander would order ten recruits from the platoon to be sent to his office, where he would interview them to determine if they had seen the drill instructor ever maltreat Private Smith. To-a-man they never saw anything. Even though they themselves had been given extra incentive training that was in violation, they always felt that the DI was only *doing his job*, and that Private Smith was the culprit. It worked every time.

On one occasion I heard of a recruit in my company that had complained that his drill instructor had struck him hard across the face with his fist. The Company Commander (CO), a former enlisted man that had also been a drill instructor, called the recruit to his office, and asked the recruit to tell what happened. After telling the CO his story the CO leaned across the desk, and hit the recruit with a very heavy blow to the face, and said: "Did your drill instructor hit you as hard as that, private?" Stunned, the recruit answered that it was. The CO looked at the recruit, and said: "Private, that was not very bad at all, so you get back to your platoon right now, and stop all this complaining nonsense!"

Good drill instructors used every means available to them to instill discipline in their recruits, but more importantly, to train them to be good Marines. The techniques seem strange to civilians, but they work for the Marine Corps. Training a person to face an enemy who is firing at him was a lot different than training someone to get along in an office environment. The recruits come into the Marine Corps fully expecting tough treatment, and they know they are not going to have an easy going. It did not take a lot of tough-love treatment to get the idea across, if they did not already know it.

One of the more colorful drill instructor characters that I have met was Master Gunnery Sergeant Bobby Biers. He tells of his time on the drill field during the Vietnam era, and brags that he never had a recruit that he did not maltreat. In fact, to be sure, on graduation night he would ask his platoons if there was any recruit that he had not called into the Duty Hut! Master Gunnery Sergeant Biers was the only drill instructor that was given a court martial hearing for maltreating twenty-nine recruits *and* his two drill instructors. He was cleared on all counts, and then received an award for being "Drill Instructor of the Quarter".

ACADEMIC
INSTRUCTION UNIT

As a recruit, any time you can get a slight break away from the drill instructors was like a slice of heaven. There was one thing in recruit training that gave recruits that break: special instruction given by the Academic Instruction Unit. There were certain classes that were of such importance that they were taught by instructors who were specialists at giving instructions to between 350 and 400 recruits at a time. History, the .45 caliber pistol, the M-14 rifle, First Aid and Hygiene were classes that required a special touch to ensure the recruits all received the same vital input. Recruits were going to be tested on that information before graduating, and they had to pass the exam to graduate.

I recall as a recruit, being marched up to the windowless classrooms—large metal buildings that contained rows and rows of metal collapsible chairs—enough chairs to seat a series of four platoons averaging eighty-five to ninety recruits per platoon. Platoon by platoon we were marched inside, and we had to stand in front of our chairs until our entire platoon was inside. We were then ordered to sit down. We could not talk. Once all four platoons were seated an instructor from the Academic Instruction Unit would take over and begin the class. Depending on the subject, the class would last from one to two hours.

History was a class that was instructed very differently than I had ever experienced while in school. The instructors put a lot of energy and enthusiasm into the presentations. The classes were made interesting, and the animated lecture was designed to instill an esperit-de-corps in the recruits. The instructors had to be dynamic for another reason too: to keep the recruits awake. The classrooms had poor ventilation, no air conditioning, and were usually pretty warm. That was compounded by the fact that the body heat from 350 recruits would further raise the building temperature.

Sometimes a recruit would fall asleep during a class. The platoon DI's were ready for that and would order the offender outside where he would be given a thorough set of incentive training exercises to waken him up. The sleepy recruit would then have to spend the rest of the class standing in the rear where the DI's stood. As if that were not enough, when the recruit got back to his Quonset hut he would be called back to the Duty Office for another chewing out and more PT. That sin would not likely be occurring again with those recruits caught nodding off.

When I became a drill instructor, the same classrooms were being used, and some of the same instructors were still giving the classes. I had learned that the instructors were themselves DI's, and were part of an elite corps of drill instructors that were hand selected to teach these important classes based on their ability to orate, and animate the subjects in a special way that recruits could learn and remember. There were two other specialty training units: Swimming Instructors who taught water survival and Hand-to-Hand Combat Instructors who taught the hand-to-hand combat and martial arts phase of the training.

After I had been on the drill field about two years I began to think of what it would be like to be a special instructor. They had a much better work schedule to work then the drill instructors had: plus, they did not have night duty, and for the most part, it was a five to six day work-week. That was very appealing. One of my favorite classes when going to school as a young man had been Speech Class, as I loved speaking to a group. So I started checking out how the process worked to get into the Academic Instructors Unit. I found out it would not be easy. First, they had to have an opening. They were also very selective and required that the drill instructor initially had to be recommended by his Commanding Officer. If the recommendation occurred the Academic Instruction Unit then held a screening process to eliminate those applicants who just wanted better duty hours from those who actually wanted to teach. Most important, they wanted a Marine who could articulate the subjects in a manner that would motivate the recruits and instill the information so that it was remembered.

I found out quickly that Marine units do not like to lose a person they value. I should have known that from the days I was at the Drill Instructor School in Parris Island, and I decided to volunteer for Vietnam duty and I was laughed out of the Headquarters Company office for even asking. When I approached my Series Commander, he was reluctant to lose me, and urged me to reconsider staying in my current drill instructor capacity. He made it clear that I was a very good drill instructor, and had a very promising future ahead of me. However hard he tried to persuade me not to change, it was apparent to him that I really wanted to give it a try and he agreed to speak to our Commanding Officer on my behalf.

Shortly after I was advised that I had been given the recommendation and was told that there was an opening at the Academic Instruction Unit (AIU) that could be applied for. At the first opportunity I went to the Noncommissioned-Officer-In-Charge (NCOIC) and applied for the job. He was really tough—he wanted to know exactly why I wanted that job. I put on my selling shoes, and told him how impressed I had been with the instructors when I was a recruit, and how much I admired their abilities to motivate the recruits with their stories and antics, and that I wanted to be involved in the process using my personality to convey the same things. I also had to go through the same process with the Officer-in-Charge (OIC). The OIC informed me that I was up against some pretty steep competition, as there were quite a few DI's that had applied, and most all of them had much more time in the Marines than I, and all had combat experience in Vietnam. Most were highly decorated Marines with many medals on their chests. He pointed out that I had less than four years in the Marines and that I only had only one ribbon on my chest. I had to really sell him on my strengths and accomplishments since being a Marine. I really stressed how badly I wanted to become an instructor.

Somehow, despite my short time in the Marines, and lack of combat experiences, I managed to beat out all the competition for the job, and I was asked to join AIU. At that point I really had my job cut out, as I had to re-learn the subjects that I would be teaching. I had to not just learn them, but to *master* them. I was assigned to bird-dog (sit with) the other instructors while they taught their classes. I had to spend endless hours rehearsing the class material, and the delivery of them. That process involved a lot of reading about Marine Corps history, first aid, as well as manuals on the weapons. I would learn that the process of teaching history was more about teaching "lore" than it was history, that the process was designed to motivate the recruits, and to instill the invincibility aspect of the Marines into their psyches. Every aspect we taught about was being "bigger than big, larger than large". Marines were portrayed as fearless warriors who could shoot more accurately than any other soldier in the world. Marines were made out to be better than any Army unit and were often portrayed as saving the Army from an enemy onslaught like what occurred in Korea. The origins of Marine nicknames such as "Leathernecks" and "Devil Dogs" were stories that instilled great pride. We also touted many famous Marine heroes such as Smedley Butler and Chesty Puller, using their stories as a means of increasing pride and heritage. Famous Marine Corps battles such as those that occurred on Tarawa, Okinawa, and Belleau Woods, were portrayed by us as epic battles that helped carve the present image of the Unites States Marines as the most feared fighting unit in the world. We also had very motivating war movies that were of actual battle scenes filmed by military cameramen.

After several weeks of studying with the other instructors, and mastering the materials, I felt I was ready. My first class was a class on History. The recruit series approached the building, and filed in, platoon after platoon, marching in-place until the DI's gave the order to halt and be seated. I could not believe how much dust was raised in that process, and how the dust rose in a cloud up to the level of the stage. Then, when everyone was seated, all eyes were on me—about *700 eyes!* Wow! That was a lot of eyes looking at me all at once. Many things go through the mind when a moment like that arrives. I was glad for the many hours of training I had put in for that, as it was now going to pay off. I took off on my subject like a duck takes to water. I threw myself into it. My apprehensions vanished after only a few moments, and I became comfortable in my new setting. As instructors, we were trained to notice how the audience was reacting—they told us by their reactions if they were listening, or, if we were dying in front of them. They were responding to my antics and oration in a very favorable way. I could tell they were comfortable with me, and that they were interested in the information I was imparting. I felt a strong sense of accomplishment with that. I even noticed the DI's at the back of the room were paying attention. I knew at the end of the presentation that I was going to make it at AIU.

I continued to pick up more classes to teach, and was instructing almost all the subjects we taught within two months. I began to master the ability to captivate an audience. Body language and oral articulation learned here would help me in other career achievements long after I left the Marine Corps.

One of our duties as an instructor with AIU was to do monitoring of other drill instructors that had to give platoon-level classes on various subjects. Those DI's would also use the same classrooms that AIU used. We would go to the classroom, and sit at the rear, and just take notes on how their delivery was, how well they knew their subjects, and we graded it accordingly. We then would file the reports to the Regimental Headquarters, and the reports would filter back down to the DI's. I was often disappointed at the level of instruction I was witnessing. Many of the DI's did not apparently spend much time, if any at all, practicing their delivery, or even studying the material beforehand, resulting in a poor presentation. While I wanted to be a good guy to these hard working Marines, I also felt it was my job to accurately report what I saw. That did not hold me in good favor with many DI's who had received a poor review, and I was subsequently referred to as "Red

Pen". I began to realize why the AIU spent so much time screening applicants: teaching subjects at this level was not for everyone.

Within a few months of having been assigned to AIU I was recommended for meritorious promotion to staff sergeant. One big problem with that was that I was not planning on re-enlisting at the end of my enlistment. My plans all along were to complete my tour of duty and then go back to civilian life. Since I would not have the required time left on my enlistment, I would not be able to accept the honor, and I had to let my superiors know that I was not planning on re-enlisting. I was a short-time Marine among "lifers"—Marines that are in it for life. Lifers thought only of the Marine Corps, and nothing else mattered much. It was hard for them to see why anyone else might not see it their way. By virtue of my being a drill instructor, and a member of the AIU at that, I was just sort of expected to be a "lifer" too. So once my intentions became known, the remaining time I had left would hold lots of extra special duties for me.

Every unit had a requirement to send some of their personnel to special training assignments: re-qualifying at the rifle range, physical fitness testing, etc. They normally do not want to send their men out, but they must. So when there was a "short-timer" in the group, he became the person that went to these functions, as that caused minimal impact on the regular duties of the unit as a whole.

Two months before I was to be discharged, I was sent to Camp Pendleton to re-qualify" with the M-14 rifle. That process was actually quite fun if we liked to shoot rifles—what Marine doesn't? So I spent a week at the rifle range—the same range the recruits qualify on. I qualified Expert on qualification day. I was happy for that, and the experience was a pleasant one.

With one more month to go in the Marine Corps, there was a need for someone to be sent to the gas chamber, so I got that call too. The *gas chamber*! Just what a person with 30 days left needs to go through for a training exercise! I remembered the gas chamber experience I had as a recruit, and could only hope and pray it would be a better experience now that I was a sergeant, and a DI at that. The group I was assigned to was sent by bus to the nearest gas chamber located at Miramar Naval Air Station, a short ride up the freeway from MCRD. We got off the bus, and met the instructors. They gave us a briefing on the gas mask, how to don it, clear it, and make sure it was sealed properly. Once they were satisfied we knew what we were doing, they had us put on the masks, and took us into the Quonset hut used for the training exercise. There was a small pot in the middle of the room and the instructor put the materials in it so it would create the gases needed. The air was quickly filling with tear gas. One by one we were approached by the instructor, and told to remove our mask, and breathe in. As we followed the order we all felt like dying an instant death! Immediately our lungs exploded, as the gas filled our lungs causing immediately coughing, gagging, and the desire to run right through the bulkhead to get clean air. Tears streamed from the eyes, snot ran like a river from the nose, and all the skin that was exposed felt like it was on fire. Our bodies were repulsing the gas, and were going into a survival mode. Air was needed, and our bodies were not getting clean air. The gas seemed to be killing us. Unlike the sadistic behavior of the troop handlers during infantry training who kept us in the Quonset hut for what seemed like an eternity, these instructors were more compassionate—they kept us in the environment for only about one minute. However, that minute seemed like an hour! After they had us put the gas mask back on and clear it, they gave the permission to exit. We gladly took them up on that, and ran outside to finally breath in some real air. It took about five to ten minutes to come back to a state of reasonable well-being. However, on the bus ride home, the gas that had also permeated our uniforms continued to emit vapors, and we were getting whiffs of tear gas. The images and feelings lingered. I took a positive outlook to all of that—I figured that somehow, some way, this might help me someday in my soon-to-be civilian life that was coming at me like a freight train. You never knew when you might come under a tear-gas attack.

One week before I was to be discharged AIU had a need to send someone out for the Physical Fitness Test. Lucky me—I got selected! So off I went, being tested for speed in the three mile run, how many pushups, pull-ups, and other exercises that were mandated by the test. By that time I was less than enthusiastic for a good score—I just wanted to get it over with.

Before a I could be discharged, I had to get a physical examination and dental check up. The Marines Corps didn't want to have a Marine discharged who needed medical or dental attention. So the last month I was in I had my physical exam—I was fine except for a significant hearing loss that I had incurred while I was in the Marines. I guess the hearing loss was mainly due to the loud jets that landed, and took off, 24 hours a day at the airport right next the MCRD, coupled with the enormous roar of recruits responding to our commands. I also had an impacted molar that a dental officer noted—he suggested they remove it. I had never used the dental services other than the original screenings we all had when we were recruits. I had heard many horror stories (I am sure they were actually unfounded) about inept Naval dentists, and how they were actually getting their internships in the Navy, having just graduated from dental schools. I was less than anxious to have them do anything, but this officer made it sound important so I agreed to have him do it. He numbed me up with Novocain, and began the process by putting what appeared to be a pliers-like instrument around the tooth to pull it out. He yanked and tugged and pulled. Then, all of a sudden I heard a loud "crunch" and the dentist said "*Damn!*" That did not sound good, but it was hard to inquire as to what the problem was when a person has a pliers-like instrument in your mouth! He finally explained that the tooth had crumbled, and he would have to perform a little surgery to clean it out. Great! I was thinking back to my original warnings about the "butchers in dental", and perhaps should have paid heed to them. Fortunately, things got better quickly, and the dentist was able to make things right, and he got all the broken pieces out. I was put on light duty for a few days while the gums heeled. I was medically cleared for a discharge at that point.

My last duty assignment in the Marines had been with the Academic Instruction Unit of the Recruit Training Regiment. I had excelled at all levels of my tenure with the Marines, and I was very proud of my achievements. On my last day I said my goodbyes to my fellow Marines, received my discharge papers, and slipped quietly out the door. As I drove through the main gate I had a tremendous feeling of both relief, and sorrow. I was relieved that I had spent close to five years in the Marine Corps during one of the most hideous wars in our nation's history, and I had escaped its enormous cruelty, fulfilling my goal of not directly participating in that ugly war. Yet, I was also leaving with an empty feeling in my gut that said I should have stayed, and made a career out of it. I would struggle with that choice for years to come.

Ironically, the gate that I first went through in getting into the Marine Corps was the very same gate I passed through upon leaving it.

Semper Fi.

PART THREE:

ONCE A MARINE, ALWAYS A MARINE

CHANGES,
BUT STILL THE SAME

Like most everything in this world, the Marine Corps slowly evolves and changes. Arguably, the changes are for the better.

A significant change since the Vietnam era Marine Corps has been the elimination of recruits handling mess duties. It was determined that civilians should be handling those duties to free up Marine manpower for more important things. That week of training time is now allocated to additional weapons training at Edson Range after the recruits have qualified with their rifles. I am sure that the additional training is important and beneficial, but I also believe that the recruits are deprived of a duty that previously built a ton of character: there was nothing like getting four or five hours of sleep, and then standing on your feet all day long to build character.

The uniforms are also a little different now. Vietnam era Marines had a utility uniform that was olive-drab and was starched heavily to maintain a certain look. The utility uniform today is a camouflage design (camos) and there are a couple of color variations using tan and green. The look of the camo uniform has a much better cut and style to it than the previous issue, and frankly, the Marines look much tougher in them than they used to. The camo utilities are no longer starched, and that in itself is an improvement to the comfort of each Marine wearing them. Another change was the elimination of the tan-colored summer dress uniform. I was saddened to see that uniform gone as it was a personal favorite while I was on active duty. The spit-shined shoes, boots and visors have been eliminated with the usage of patent leather for the shoes and visors, and tan rough-out boots that do not require shining.

The whole organizational structure of the recruit platoons and companies has also changed. There used to be four platoons in a series. There would be several series in a company. Each series had a Series Gunnery Sergeant and a Series Officer who were the senior NCO and officer of the series. The company had a Company

Commander, typically a captain. Today the series are set up like a standard Marine Corps Company, utilizing a First Sergeant as the senior company Staff NCO. That makes more sense because the recruits will eventually be assigned to a regular company. Each company also now has a Navy Corpsman, allowing the recruits to get much quicker medical attention when needed than the old days.

The training syllabus is also different. Less time is devoted to drill, and more time has been dedicated to core values, and leadership. The whole Marine Corps philosophy has been upgraded in this area to stress Marines making the right decisions. This stems from the Marines now utilizing more leadership from junior members who operate in smaller groups in combat situations. Wars are now fought a little differently than they were in the Vietnam era, and the Marines have changed to address these differences.

The drill instructors are a little different now too. It is an all-volunteer force, unlike the Vietnam era when some Marines were ordered to attend DI school if they met the minimum criteria. The drill instructor candidates must now show financial stability. They appear more physically fit than previous eras. They also are much more closely monitored to ensure that the SOP (Standard Operating Procedures) is adhered to. There are more senior officers and senior Staff NCOs monitoring events.

The Quonset huts are now gone except for a dozen that the Depot Museum kept for historic showings. The recruits are now housed in barracks. The barracks provide a much better environment to monitor recruit activities. Many of the older training facilities have also been upgraded, and made much more modern. The Receiving Barracks, Medical Offices, and the recruit PX, have been replaced with new buildings. There is now a new modern Obstacle Course for the recruits to run. Clothing issue has been moved to a brand new building that is a major improvement from the old metal buildings that were very hot and muggy.

The two parades that the Vietnam era recruits participated in are now down to a single parade, and that parade is now part of the graduation ceremony. At the end of the graduation ceremony the recruits are now immediately dismissed, and sent on a 10 day leave before they report to infantry training at the School of Infantry located at Camp Pendleton. Graduation also is open to the public, and the recruits' families are encouraged to attend. The ceremony now a very larger event and significant crowds come to the graduations that are held most every Friday. In addition to the Friday graduations, the families are invited to attend other activities on the Thursday before graduation. The recruits are given base liberty that day in the afternoon, and are free to visit with their families. With the advent of the computer age, the families have a greater access to the process by looking up on line, the training schedules, and information about the training events. Families are urged to purchase tee shirts, hats, and other memorabilia to show support for their Marine.

Technology has improved almost all of the equipment the Marine Corps uses now as well. DI's have computers to keep track of the records they are required to keep regarding every recruit. In the old days, we used a 5 X 8 card, and scribbled notes on the backs of the cards, stapling one card on top of another as they were needed. Almost all of the gear recruits are issued now is significantly better than the Vietnam era. The gear is of better quality, lighter in weight, and easier to use.

Recruit fluid intake is closely monitored now, and they are required to ingest certain minimum amounts of fluids to avoid dehydration. Dehydration used to be a common problem resulting in muscle cramps, constipation, and other issues. They are allowed to eat their meals in a more stress-free environment than we used to create for them.

A new and very big upgrade to training was the addition of "The Crucible" which is an intense, four day session that is the most grueling part of boot camp training. Recruits go on a forced march with a full array of field gear that weighs around eight-five pounds. They will be limited to eating a small ration of food. In addition, recruits will participate in many drills that are designed to require them to exercise teamwork. During this event they find out what being a Marine is really all about. There will be night shooting exercises, and exposure to war-like activities. It is the pinnacle point of recruit training, and it is considered the defining moment in the training cycle. Once the Crucible is completed, the recruits are considered to be Marines. After the four days out in the field the recruits are physically exhausted, and totally spent. Upon arriving back to the base camp they are treated to a special meal, and due to the limited rations they had during the Crucible, the meal is probably one of the best they can ever remember at any time in their lives. This is probably one of the single biggest and most important changes in the training cycle.

The Grinder is now smaller in dimension than it used to be. They have taken up some of the Grinder for parking. Upon first look I was really surprised at how much smaller it appeared with all the cars parking in the old marching areas. However, I doubt that a recruit will notice the smaller size when he is marching the length of the Grinder holding an M-16 rifle at port arms the whole time. Another change on the Grinder is the inclusion of bleachers on both sides of the Reviewing Stand. These bleachers are now used for the family members who come to witness the recruit graduations, and are usually full from the top to their bottoms on graduation day.

Another significant change today is the way that the Marines are recognized by the public. Although the Marines never have had a public-image problem, during the Vietnam era all members of the military received undue haranguing by civilians. Military personnel during the Vietnam era were viewed by civilians, and the protesting youth in particular, with disdain, and the public would display their disdain by spitting on them or calling them "baby killers". It was not a comfortable thing for a Marine to be in uniform during those times because of the negative attention it could bring. Today, Marines are applauded at every occasion and their image has become that of being the "911" force for the US. I recall being at a baseball game in San Diego the week-end after the events of September 11, 2001. America was still in a pall over the tragedy in New York earlier in the week. It so happened that a graduating recruit company was in attendance at the ball park to see the game. The teletron camera was panning the audience, as it normally does during lulls in the game's activity, when it came to the Marine recruits in the stands with their drill instructors. The moment the audience saw the Marines on the jumbotron screen they jumped to their feet, and erupted into a non-stop standing ovation that lasted over ten minutes. Even the players were standing there applauding the Marines! More amazing was when the recruits got up to leave at the end of the seventh inning—all eyes were on them as they passed trash bags amongst their ranks to collect all their trash, and carry it out with them. The game was now a forgotten thing with the audience as they were focused solely on the Marines. Then the recruits filed out of the stadium to fall into platoon formations just outside the structure. The audience filed outside with them and formed a huge gauntlet from the stadium down to the area the recruit busses were parked. As the recruits marched by, the audience cheered and applauded. It was an amazing sight to behold.

The Marine Corps training environment has definitely improved and the recruits have it much better than ever in the past. But, to old salts such as myself, and the peers I worked with, the "Old Corps" seemed much tougher.

A MARINE EVER AFTER

I do not know who coined the phrase "once a Marine, always a Marine", but it is absolutely true. It is impossible to erase the discipline learned in recruit training and the leadership encountered throughout the Marine Corps during any Marine's tenure, no matter how long or short it may have been. It is a life-changing event for most men who go through Marine Corps boot camp. The images of their drill instructors are etched forever in their minds. I can still hear my DI's calling their drill cadence, and would recognize their voices in a crowd of people in an instant. There is no way to erase their images, the impact was so great.

Having been a drill instructor myself I knew the impact we were having on recruits. At the end of each platoon, on their last day of boot camp, we would have them write a critique of us and their training. They knew there would be no retaliation and they were encouraged to be honest. Despite the harshness of the treatment, and the many things they endured, they always came up with very inspiring thoughts about us. They appreciated the tough handling and constant badgering, as they came to realize that they were better off for having been able to endure the toughest training regimen of all the military services. Almost to a man the common theme was that they came into the Marine Corps and *wanted to become a man*. They knew the Marine Corps builds men. The harsher the treatment they received, the more they appreciated their achievements. They were going to be taking those images and memories with them into the Marine Corps and those disciplines would last their lifetimes.

When I left the Marine Corps I felt that I had accomplished something really special. In my particular case I had also achieved the ultimate reward of having been a drill instructor. That job was considered the best job a Marine can have while in the Marines and only the top few percent of the Marine NCOs are even eligible. So I had a more unique view on being a Marine than many who did not experience what I had.

I entered civilian life and went into sales. My first experience with civilians was with a multi-level marketing company. I had risen to one of their management positions before I had even gotten out of the Marines, as I had started on a part-time basis while I was still in the Corps. But almost immediately I noticed there was a significant difference from what I was used to: civilians did not *respond* the same way as Marines did. Civilians didn't react to orders. I had just spent three years with people jumping instantly when I barked an order, and that was something I had grown to expect. It took a long time for me to get used to the difference between civilians and Marines.

The leadership training and experience I had in the Marine Corps would propel me through to the highest levels in most organizations I would work for during the remainder of my civilian career. I had always been a get-up-and-go sort of guy before I enlisted, but the Marine experience definitely made it a life-long way of doing things.

After I was discharged I continued to miss the Marine Corps and its discipline. In civilian life you really don't know where you stand within an organization. There are no rank insignia in civilian life. You can't tell at a glance who is a senior person, and it is often dog-eat-dog. I have managed to do well and I ultimately ended up in the mortgage business. About twenty two years after I last drove out of the main gate of MCRD I had achieved the position of being the president of a mortgage company. One day one of my loan officers came to me and said a gentleman in his office was a retired Marine Sergeant Major who had been a drill instructor at MCRD. He said that as soon as the client was told that I too had been a DI he wanted to speak to me. As a courtesy, I stepped into the office and introduced myself. The client was a bull-dog of a man and he stood up and shook my hand and introduced himself as retired Sergeant Major Bill Paxton. He was so full of energy and enthusiasm! He asked me if I had heard of the Marine Corps Drill Instructors Association. I told him I had not and he went on to tell me all about it. He had been one of the original members when it was started in the 1980's. It was a group of DI's, mostly retired, that had successfully been through at least one tour of duty on the drill field. A big light went off in my head. For the past twenty-odd years I had an empty place in my soul where the Marine Corps had once filled the space. Maybe the DI Association could be the thing that would fill that void. I gave him my address, and he said he would mail me an application. His enthusiasm was endless!

A few days later I received a package in the mail that included an application for the Drill Instructor Association membership. I chose to be a life-time member and completed the application and sent in my check for the lifetime dues. I felt like I had just re-enlisted in the Marine Corps! I finally had a connection again. A week or so later I received my membership card and information about the upcoming reunion. Every three months I would receive a newsletter. Unfortunately, my schedule was such that I did not attend the reunions for the first couple of years that I was a member. Finally, I got a break in my workload, and was able to attend a DI reunion.

The first reunion I attended started off with a breakfast at the mess hall. Wow, what a treat! My wife was with me and that was her first official Marine Corps breakfast. I couldn't believe my eyes when I went through the mess line: the food looked *exactly* the same way as it had twenty-five years earlier! There was the same SOS, scrambled eggs, and the toast that was neither really toasted, nor warm. There were also the pancakes that seemed to have been cooked the morning before, and choices of sausage or bacon. The sausages were exactly like they used to be: almost browned. We all sat in a special area in the mess hall that had been reserved for the association members. There were many current drill instructors present, as well as men that had been on the drill field as far back as World War II. I looked around to see if I could recognize anyone I might have known from my time on the field. I did not recognize anyone. The Association President, retired Master Sergeant Mike West, took the floor and gave a speech about what the activities for the day were going to be. Then we heard from the Regimental Sergeant Major, and finally the Deport Sergeant Major. It was all very impressive. What really stood out to me was the enthusiasm those Marines had for sharing and remembering their experiences of their pasts as DI's. The stories that were being told put me mentally right back on the drill field.

Soon I recognized Sergeant Major Bill Paxton and re-introduced myself, and thanked him for giving me the opportunity to join the Association. He was still so enthusiastic and full of vitality. I noticed that he was also the center of a lot of attention from the other Marines present. I would learn more about him as time went on. He is one of the most colorful Marines I have ever met. He is an endless story of achievement and involvement.

I would later find out that SgtMaj Paxton attended almost every event he could that involved the Marine Corps. He had been president of the Marine Corps League and was still actively involved. He often tells the story of when he and his junior drill instructor caught two recruits smoking in the heads one night. They took them outside and ordered them to jump into a dipsy-dumpster then told them to smoke a large cigar while the dumpster cover was closed—a technique sure to end their desire to ever smoke again. He told his junior drill instructor to take them out in an hour or so, and put them back with the platoon. He then went about his nightly business. The next morning SgtMaj Paxton learned that his junior drill instructor had received bad news upon returning to the duty hut minutes after putting the two privates in the dumpster, and he had to go on emergency leave immediately. He was informed that the two privates were missing. SgtMaj Paxton immediately ran out to retrieve the recruits, only to discover the dumpster was already picked up and taken to the dump so the trash inside could be emptied. Like a madman he raced to the dump to prevent a tragedy. When he arrived he was told it was too late, that the dumpster had caught fire and a fire crew was present to extinguish the blaze. He saw his whole career going up in smoke, and was trying to figure out what he could possibly say to explain this tragedy to his commanding officer. Soon he was informed that the fire captain, a former Marine, had spotted the recruits outside the dumpster and had them put into detainment. That was probably the only time in SgtMaj Paxton's entire career that he was actually worried, and a little scared. He would later learn that one of those recruits was *Ken Norton*, a man who became the heavy weight boxing champion of the world.

SgtMaj Paxton also told a story about his son who was also in the Marines. His son graduated from boot camp the same day SgtMaj Paxton retired: he was part of the graduation ceremony and he was given special recognition for his services during the retirement ceremony. His son would later leave the Marine Corps and join the San Diego Police Department. His son would also become famous during the infamous tank chase that took place in San Diego: a distraught Army reservist stole a tank from the Army Reserve Armory tank compound, and began to create holy terror driving down city streets, running over cars, motor homes, and taking out anything in the path of the tank. It was a major live news event with helicopters showing the tanks' every move. Nothing could stop that tank. The renegade drove the tank onto the freeway and attempted to drive over cars, and even tried to take out a bridge. Finally, with about 100 police cars in a hopeless pursuit, the tank driver attempted to cross the cement barrier between the northbound and southbound lanes. The vehicle got high centered on the barrier and the tank was stalled in place. It was still very dangerous. Paxton's son was familiar with tanks due to his Marine Corps background, and he knew how to open the tank's hatches. He jumped up onto the dangerous tank while it was being jerked left and right. Using a bolt cutter, he opened the hatch and ordered the driver to cease his actions. The driver ignored young Paxton, so Paxton pulled his revolver out of his holster and shot the man in a desperate attempt to end the fiasco. The man died shortly after from the gunshot. Paxton was a hero. It was later noted that the tank was chased by hundreds of police officers, but it took just *one Marine* to stop the tank!

Following the reunion breakfast we were ushered to the Depot Headquarters area and given front-row seats for the Friday Color Ceremonies. The Commanding General and his staff have a morning ceremony each Friday that involved the colors being raised. It was a very colorful event that included the band playing very patriotic marching music. There was a large audience of recruit parents and family members who were there for the day's graduation ceremonies that we were going to see in another hour or two. I was sucking up every minute of that.

After the ceremony was over a group picture taken was of all the members present, and then we headed off for a tour of the Drill Instructor School. At the school there were pictures of all the graduating classes going back well into the early 1950's. I looked through the whole group of pictures and could not locate my DI class picture on the wall. That was a low point for me as I really wanted my wife Melody to see that picture. We were given a briefing about the school by the Chief Drill Instructor, First Sergeant Dave Francisco. He was typical of a senior staff NCO—solid, well built and full of military bearing. A year or so after that reunion, 1st Sgt Francisco would be the lead man in a reality television show called "Celebrity Boot Camp". The show used real Marine Corps drill instructors that were in charge of civilians who were all on a training mission. The program was on TV for about 12 weeks and they eliminated one civilian person each week. The show was about using Marine Corps training techniques on civilians. The civilians did not fare well with the drill instructors in their faces constantly. First Sergeant Francisco would later tell a story of how the producers wanted the Marine DI's to create a script to follow when they were doing their DI acts toward the civilians. The DI's all laughed at the producers, and advised them that drill instructors do not "script their acts": it was real and genuine and comes from within. It was a natural thing for all DI's. There were no scripted DI acts in the Marine Corps boot camp environment.

First Sergeant Francisco's orientation at the school described what the process of training DI's was and how it probably had changed from the time we were on the drill field. I noticed many significant changes in policies. I might not have had the same chance today that I had in my time and I began to be thankful I went through when I did. One thing was still clear: Drill Instructor School is still one of the most grueling, disciplined, and prestigious courses in the Marine Corps.

Once the DI School tour was over we were free for an hour or so before we had to convene at the Parade Deck bleachers to view a recruit graduation ceremony and parade. My wife and I decided to go to the Depot Museum and see the exhibits there. We strolled through the building and eagerly viewed each display. We came to a display about the Drill Instructors School—and there, on the wall, was a photo of the Drill Instructor School class of December, 1969: my DI School class! It was a real thrill to see that photo of my old friends, and to also to be memorialized in the museum. By that time I was ready to re-enlist.

The parade and graduation ceremony was another thrill for the reunion attendees. The band played music, and the parade brought back many memories of the parades that we had participated in while we were recruits and drill instructors on the field. The graduation ceremonies were now part of the parade process— quite a change from when I was on the field when the graduation took place in the theater at the end of the Parade Deck. The DI Association had a reserved bleacher located next to the Reviewing Stand. We were given special recognition during the ceremonies.

After the parade, a barbeque lunch was on the agenda. Off to the boathouse we all went where the barbeque was held. There were several hundred members, both active duty and old timers such as myself, at the barbeque. After a great meal they held a cadence-calling contest, with one for the old salts and another for the active duty DI's. Here I saw SgtMaj Paxton display his cadence calling ability—he won the old salts side hands down. He was turning out to be quite a character I was finding. An auction was held to make money for the Association and it was conducted by previous Sergeant Major of the Marine Corps, retired Sergeant Major Summers. Many donated Marine Corps items were auctioned off, and the proceeds all went into the coffers for student scholarships.

My wife Melody and I decided to tour the base. What a treat—it was exactly as it was during my stay on the field, except that the Quonset huts had now been replaced by more modern barracks that had been under construction while I was still on the field. I was disappointed to see that the Quonset huts that I had lived in now gone. But there were still about a dozen Quonset huts that the Depot Museum maintained to preserve the memories of how it used to be. We drove past the drill field and stopped to listen to the drill instructors teaching drill—nothing seemed to have changed since I had been on the field except the uniforms were now camos and the recruits were using M-16 rifles instead of the M-14's we used to carry. As we watched, I was able to point out the errors the recruits were making to my wife, and almost as soon as I would point them out the drill instructors would get all over those particular recruits for the same reasons. I know beyond a shadow of doubt that I could have stepped on the field and taken over a platoon and not skipped a beat!

We were so impressed with the event that we decided to come the next day to a special ceremony that would honor the unveiling of the Marine Corps Drill Instructor Memorial—this was a special memorial that had been years in the making. I would learn that the person most responsible for that memorial was none other than SgtMaj Bill Paxton! He saw a need to have a monument to honor those Marine drill instructors that were no longer with us, and he lobbied with his typical enthusiasm to every possible source that could assist that to happen. The monument statues consisted of one male drill instructor and one female drill instructor. There would be two such monuments, one in San Diego, and the other at Parris Island. At the bases of the monuments are special bricks that members could purchase and have their names engraved on them. Proceeds from the brick sales went to assist in the cost of the memorial. I was determined to have my name on a brick.

The unveiling ceremony was very impressive. There were about one hundred active-duty DI's present and another 150 or so Association members. The band played marching music, and there was a bugle corps to play Taps. Sergeant Major Paxton gave a very moving eulogy for the fallen Marines and named each by name. There was a bell toll for each name called. When it was over Taps was played by the two buglers, and ended with a twenty-one gun salute. Everyone there was very moved by the ceremony. Also present was movie star R. Lee Ermey, the actor who played the leading drill instructor role in the movie "Full Metal Jacket". Ermey was also a Marine drill instructor in the mid 1960's and he scripted the scenes for the boot camp scenes from his memories of his time as a drill instructor. He was an active member of the Marine Corps Drill Instructors Association.

There was still a banquet dinner scheduled, but unfortunately, my wife and I could not attend that evening event. However, we vowed to attend all the events for the next reunion. After arriving home I had a hollow feeling in my stomach—I wanted more!

The Association had brought me back into the Marine Corps loop. I felt like I had arrived once more. My wife and I started to attend more Friday graduations and taking in a tour of the base on each occasion. Each time it felt like coming home again.

The following year we attended all the events of the reunion. It was truly grand. I was beginning to meet many new friends, and I found many DI's that I had either been on the field at the same time with, or they were from that era. I was beginning to see a trend here—almost all of the Marines in the Association felt exactly like I did—they all wanted to come back and smell the smells, feel the boot camp pulse, hear the sounds, and be a part of it all over again. We all felt like we could still be drill instructors, if only they would let us.

The Association was full of some of the most dynamic leaders and characters that the Marine Corps had produced in those eras. I would soon learn than many of the members were often Sergeants Major or Master Gunnery Sergeants with a few Master Sergeants and First Sergeants. I was once again the "junior-man" of the group. I have never been around more Sergeants Major in my whole life.

I have met many very colorful Marines in the Association, but some really stand out. Master Gunnery Sergeant Bobby Biers was one of the most feisty and outspoken members of the group. He was one of the original members, and was assigned the task of getting new members to join. One of his claims to fame was that he underwent a court-martial for maltreating his entire platoon *and two of his drill instructors!* Master Gunnery Sergeant Biers was an endless story and very interesting to listen to. First Sergeant James Wilson was another example of outstanding leadership—he was Company First Sergeant of Fox Company, Second Recruit Training Battalion, and at the time I met him, the President of the Crow Crawford Chapter of the Drill Instructor Association. At one point he had increased the membership to over 500 members locally. I witnessed his leadership ability during one very fiery meeting of the members in which some of the audience was treating 1st Sgt Wilson and his Depot peers with considerable contempt for their raising some questions about the handling of Association affairs by the present officers of the national headquarters of the association. He calmly stood his ground, and despite his more junior rank to the many sergeants major in the audience, remained calm under the continuous pressure from the group. I was so impressed with his ability to handle that pressure that I later approached him and gave him my business card, and invited him to call me whenever he retired so I could give him a job as a loan officer. Several years later he retired from the Marine Corps, and he tracked me down. I hired him on the spot—he turned out to be my top loan officer. We have remained friends ever since.

The Marine Corps Drill Instructor Association was like any large group— over time there were differences of opinion as to how things should be run. The Association president, Mike West, had been President of the Marine Corps Drill Instructors Association since its inception. There were some members that felt it was time for a change, and they started to find irregularities in the handling of things. There began a splintering of the group, and some members felt it was time for the president to step aside. The whole drama created quite a furor among members, and the political aspect of the organization began to take over the common sense side of it. For about two years the Association sort of floated along while charges were thrown back and forth. As a result, there were some members who were banned from the Association due to their involvement in the challenges to the authority. It really created a rift in the group as a whole.

Vic Ditchkoff was voted in as the new national president after Mike West stepped aside. The healing process was beginning. The local chapter in San Diego was named the Crow Crawford Chapter after retired Sergeant Major of the Marine Corps, Crow Crawford, who was the person most responsible for starting the Association in the first place. The Crow Crawford Chapter was now without officers. The last evening of the 2006 reunion I was asked to become an officer of the Crow Crawford Chapter. To me it was an honor and I gladly accepted.

My first meeting with the Association took place at the Drill Instructor School conference room. In the meeting was the Deport Sergeant Major, SgtMaj Bobby Woods, and the person SgtMaj Woods selected to be the president, retired SgtMaj Dave Francisco: the same Dave Francisco that had previously been the Chief Drill Instructor at the Drill Instructor School when I took a tour of the facility on my first reunion. I was asked to be the Secretary. SgtMaj Woods made it clear that he wanted to put behind us the rift we had gone through, and bring the Association back to the premier status it had in the past. We made plans for the upcoming reunion which was scheduled a few months away. It seemed that no matter what I did with the Marine Corps I always seemed to end up at the top of things!

Today I do not walk out of my house without some sign of the Marine Corps on my person—a pin, a cap, a shirt, or all of them. I am proud of the time I spent with the Marine Corps, and I realize how great the experience really was. I am also proud of my current status with the DI Association, and the new friendships and associations I now have with so many highly decorated, and devoted men. It is truly an honor for me.

In a recent meeting the Depot Sergeant Major, expressed a desire to have the Drill Instructor Association spearhead a movement to get a memorial of Iwo Jima installed by the Depot flag pole that is at the center of the east side of the parade deck. That was the sort of project that the DI Association could easily accomplish due to the large base of leaders within the organization.

Once a Marine, always a Marine. Semper Fi!

GLOSSARY

ALIGNMENT: The left-to-right straightness of rows in formations

AS YOU WERE!: Resume what you were doing

ASSHOLES AND ELBOWS: In a hurry; quickly

AWOL: Absent without leave

BENDS AND THRUSTS: The most hated exercise recruits get; often used for incentive training PT

BILLET: Assignment of job; place of residence

BLOUSE: noun: Jacket; verb: to tuck in; secure

BLOUSING BANDS: Elastic bands used to secure utility trouser cuffs on boots

BOOT: Recruit

BRAIN HOUSING GROUP: The brain or mind

BRIG: Jail

BULKHEAD: Wall

BUTT: The target mechanism used to hold the targets at the rifle range

BUTTS: The target area at the rifle range

CIVVIES: Civilian clothes

BUCKET ISSUE: Initial issue of all items a recruit will need to start book camp

BY-YOUR-LEAVE: A request of an enlisted man to pass an officer; a request of a recruit to pass a drill instructor or officer

BY-THE-NUMBERS: In sequence

CAMOS: Camouflage utility uniform

CAMPAIGN COVER: The drill instructor hat; Smokey-the-bear hat; the Hat

CARRY ON!: Continue what you were doing; as you were

CATTLE CAR: A trailer used for hauling military personnel and their gear; looks like a trailer used for hauling cattle

CG: Commanding General

CHIT: An authorization

CHOW: Food

CHOW HALL: Mess hall

CIVILIAN: Anyone other than a military person

CO: Commanding officer

COLORS: The flag; a ceremony of raising or lowering of the flag

COMPANY: One of several units in a Battalion;

C-RATIONS: Canned field rations

CORKY'S: The worst eatery anywhere; found around the corner from the Los Angeles Military Processing Center

CORPSMAN: A Navy medic that serves with the Marines

COVER: noun: A hat verb: alignment of one person behind another

CHOKE YOURSELF: A suggestion to a recruit, that he take the hand of his drill instructor, and use it to choke himself as a disciplinary measure

DECK: Floor; ground

DI: Short for drill instructor

DI'S GRASS: Any dirt around the barracks or Quonset hut and is considered sacred

DITTY BAG: A small cloth bag with a draw string used to hold dirty clothes

DIDDY BOP: A certain swagger; an attitude of walk

DOGGIE: An army person

DRAFTEE: A person that was inducted into the military by the Selective Service

DRILL INSTRUCTOR: The trainer of recruits; DI; a god-like figure

DUTY: Time required being on the job; in charge; job assignment

DUTY HUT: A drill instructors Quonset hut; a duty office

DUTY OFFICE: A drill instructors office

DUTY NCO: The non-commissioned officer in-charge at each unit each day

ENLISTEE: A person that voluntarily joined the military

EYEBALL: To scrutinize; to gaze at

FARTSACK: A mattress cover

FIELD DAY: A general or thorough cleaning of a barracks

FIELD STRIP: To disassemble; take apart

FIRST PHASE: The first phase of recruit training

FOOT LOCKER: The wooden box each Marine has under his rack to store his gear

GANG WAY!: Step aside; make room

GEAR: Equipment

GI CAN: A trash can; sometimes highly polished in recruit barracks

GRABASS: Horseplay; goofing off; playing around

GRINDER: Parade deck

GUIDE: The man in front of the platoon formation that carries the Gideon; the recruit in charge of the platoon in the drill instructors absence

GUIDEON: A pennant attached to a staff that gives the unit designation; carried by the Guide

GUNNEY: A gunnery sergeant

HAT: Drill Instructor; cover

HATCH: Door

HEAD: Toilet

HEAD-CALL: A trip to the toilet

HOUSE MOUSE: The drill instructors' maid or go-fer

HONCHO: Boss; man in charge

"I": A term a recruit cannot ever call themselves

IN YOUR FACE: The act of getting up-close and yelling directly at the recruit

INCENTIVE TRAINING: Extra physical training imposed for infractions or lack of motivation

IRISH PENNANT: A loose string on a uniform; any loose item such as sheets protruding from under a rack

ITR: Infantry Training Regiment

JARHEAD: A Marine

JUNIOR DRILL INSTRUCTOR: drill instructor junior to the platoon commander

JUNK-ON-THE-BUNK: An inspection requiring all of a Marines' gear to be laid out on a bunk in a formal lay-out

LEAVE: An authorized absence over twenty-four hours

LIBERTY: Time off less than 24 hours

LIFER: A Marine that is in for a life

LOCK AND LOAD: Arm and ready your weapon; get ready

MAGGIES' DRAWERS: A red flag flown over a target when the shooter has missed the target completely

MANUAL OF ARMS: Drill movements involving the rifle; rifle movements

MESS HALL: An eating facility; chow hall

M-14: Standard rifle issue during the Vietnam era

MCRD: Marine Corps Recruit Depot

MILITARY TIME: Twenty-four hour clock: starts at 0001 and runs through 2400 each day; does not require the use of AM or PM to identify morning and afternoon

MOS: Military occupational specialty

MUSTANG: An officer that was a former enlisted man

NCO: Non-commissioned officer

NCOIC: Non-commissioned officer-in-charge

NON-QUAL: A Marine that fails to qualify with the weapon at the rifle range

OFFICE POGUE: A desk-bound Marine

OFFICER-OF-THE-DAY: The duty officer each day at all commands

OIC: Officer-in-charge

OUTSTANDING!: Job well done; exceptional

OVERHEAD: Ceiling

OVERLAP: The overlapping of schedules of graduating platoons and incoming platoons

OVER THE HILL: Unauthorized absence

PARADE DECK: The grinder; used for marching and ceremonies

PARRIS ISLAND: Island in South Carolina that MCRD is located at

PASSAGEWAY: A corridor or hallway

PI: Parris Island

PIT: The designated location for doing incentive training PT

PHYSICAL TRAINING: Exercising activity; PT

PLATOON: Made up of four squads; eighty-five to ninety men (Vietnam era)

PLATOON COMMANDER: The senior drill instructor; wears a shiny black leather duty belt

POGEY BAIT: Candy; sweets

POLICE CALL: The time allocated to clean up an area

POLICE UP: To clean up

PT: Physical training

PUGIL STICK: A heavily padded pole used in hand-to-hand combat training to simulate rifle and bayonet fighting

QUONSET HUT: A metal building with a round non-stop roof; used for recruit billeting during the Vietnam War era

QUARTERS: Living space

RACK: Bunk; bed

RECEIVING BARRACKS: The place recruits initially start at when arriving at MCRD

REVEILLE: Time to get up in the morning

RIFLE RANGE: The place where Marines learn to shoot their weapons

ROUND: Bullet

RTB: Recruit Training Battalion

RTR: Recruit Training Regiment

SALT: An experienced Marine

SALTY: Having an attitude; opinionated

SAND FLEA: A small flea that creates a living hell for Parris Island recruits

SEABAG: A duffel bag used to carry ones' possessions

SEA LAWYER: a person who thinks he has all the answers; know-it-all

SEA STORY: A big story; an exaggeration

SECOND PHASE: Second phase of recruit training; time at the rifle range; period for mess and maintenance week

SECURE: to put things in there place; to tie something down; to stop doing something

SERIES: Four platoons that proceed through boot camp as a unit (Vietnam era)

SERIES GUNNY: The gunnery sergeant in a recruit series who is in charge

SERIES OFFICER: The officer of a recruit series

SEVEN-EIGHTY TWO GEAR (782): Field equipment; canvas gear issue

SHIT BIRD: A screw-up; a messy or undisciplined person

SHORT TIMER: A Marine with a short time left on their enlistment

SICK BAY: A medical clinic or hospital

SICK BAY COMMANDO: A person that goes to sick bay

SIGHTING IN: Adjusting the sights of the rifle to hit the target at various distances

SKIPPER: A captain; commanding officer

SKIVVIES: Underwear

SMOKING LAMP: The authority to smoke when it is lit

SNAPPING-IN: Practicing shooting the rifle without rounds; practicing trigger-squeeze

SOP: Standard Operating Procedure; a standard set of rules for handling recruits that covers all situations

SPIT SHINE: Super-glossy shine on boots or shoes

SQUAD: One row of four that each platoon was made up of

SQUAD BAY: Barracks

SQUAD LEADER: The person in charge of the squad; stands at the front of the platoon with other squad leaders, behind the guide

SQUARED AWAY: Neat; organized; orderly

STAND BY: Prepare

STANDBY: Waiting status

STARCHIES: Starched utility uniform

SURVEY: Dispose of; eliminate

SWAB: Mop

SWABBY: A sailor

TAPS: The time lights go out; time for bed

THIRD PHASE: Final phase of training

THUMPING: Touching a recruit; maltreatment; violation of the SOP

TOP: Short name for master sergeant; first sergeant; sergeant major

TOPSIDE: Above; upstairs

TURN TO!: Begin work

UA: Unauthorized absence

UTILITIES: Olive drab field uniform

YELLOW FOOTPRINTS: Painted yellow footprints that mark the spot recruit's first stand on after exiting the bus upon arrival at MCRD; the starting point of boot camp; the beginning of hell for a period of time; footprints etched in the minds of every Marine

"YOU": A term a recruit can never call a drill instructor

ZERO-DARK-THIRTY: Very early in the morning; before sunrise

CPSIA information can be obtained at www.ICGtesting.com
Printed in the USA
BVOW05s0205241214

380772BV00001B/30/P